CHILDHOOD TRAUMA FOR KIDS 9-12

MASTER YOUR PAST WOUNDS, GET HEALED, STOP FEELING STUCK AND COPE UP WITH PTSD THROUGH CBT

By

Carol C.

Serene Publications

Disclaimer Notice

This book is written and published independently. Please keep in mind that the material in this publication is solely for educational and entertaining purposes. All efforts have provided authentic, up-to-date, trustworthy, and comprehensive information. There are no express or implied assurances. The purpose of this book's material is to assist readers in having a better understanding of the subject matter. The activities, information, and exercises are provided solely for self-help information. This book is not intended to replace expert psychologists, legal, financial, or other guidance. If you require counseling, please get in touch with a qualified professional.

By reading this text, the reader accepts that the author will not be held liable for any damages, indirectly or directly, experienced due to the use of the information included herein, particularly, but not limited to, omissions, errors, or inaccuracies. You are accountable for your decisions, actions, and consequences as a reader.

About the Author

Dr. Carol C. is a distinguished psychologist, published author, and dynamic motivational speaker, with over 15 years of specialized experience in the treatment of childhood trauma, Post-Traumatic Stress Disorder (PTSD), and related mental health issues. Dr. Carol C's multifaceted approach is grounded in the belief that every child and teenager possesses untapped potential and unique strengths, waiting to be unlocked. Through her cutting-edge therapeutic techniques, empowering workshops, and compassionate guidance, she helps young people from all walks of life to overcome adversity, and transform their lives from surviving to thriving.

TABLE OF CONTENTS

FEW WORDS FOR RISING STARS 7

INTRODUCTION...8

CHAPTER 1: UNDERSTANDING CHILDHOOD TRAUMA
.... 11

1.1. Unraveling The Mystery of Childhood Trauma 12

1.2. The Many Faces of Childhood Trauma................................13

1.3. The Ripple Effects of Trauma 14

1.4. How Trauma Can Lead to PTSD.......................................15

CHAPTER 2: RECOGNIZING YOUR CHILD'S TRAUMA
SYMPTOMS 17

2.1. The Hidden Wounds: Common Symptoms of Childhood Trauma in
Children 17

2.2. When Trauma Speaks Louder: How Trauma Can Affect Your Child's
Thoughts, Feelings, and Behaviors 19

2.3. Flashbacks and Triggers: Understanding Triggers and Flashbacks in
Children 20

2.4 Ventures 21

CHAPTER 3: THE ROLE OF CBT IN HEALING
CHILDHOOD TRAUMA.. 30

3.1. Unlocking The Power of CBT: A Comprehensive Guide 30

3.2. The Healing Power of CBT: A Proven Method for Overcoming
Childhood Trauma..32

3.3. The ABCs of Healing: How CBT's ABC Model Helps Your Child Identify and Change Negative Thought Patterns 40

3.4. Ventures..41

CHAPTER 4: HELPING YOUR CHILD CHALLENGE NEGATIVE THOUGHTS AND BELIEFS 45

4.1. Uncovering The Roots of Negative Thoughts and Beliefs in Your Child 45

4.2. Weighing the Evidence: Challenging Negative Thoughts and Beliefs with Facts...46

4.3. Empowering Your Child: Techniques to Replace Negative Thoughts with Positive Ones 48

4.4. Ventures..49

CHAPTER 5: SUPPORTING YOUR CHILD'S COPING STRATEGIES FOR MANAGING TRAUMA SYMPTOMS ..55

5.1. Breathing Exercises...55

5.2. Mindfulness Practices 56

5.3. Grounding Techniques 57

5.4. Self-Soothing Strategies 59

5.5. Ventures..59

CHAPTER 6: SUPPORTING YOUR CHILD IN OVERCOMING FEAR AND AVOIDANCE 68

6.1. Understanding Avoidance Behaviors in Children................................68

6.2. Gradual Exposure to Feared Situations...69

6.3. Practicing Relaxation Techniques During Exposure 70

6.4. Ventures **71**

CHAPTER 7: BUILDING POSITIVE RELATIONSHIPS WITH YOUR CHILD **82**

7.1. Broken Bonds: How Childhood Trauma Can Damage Relationships in Adulthood **82**

7.2. Building Positive Relationships with Your Child **83**

7.3. Developing Healthy Boundaries **84**

7.4. Ventures **86**

CHAPTER 8: ENCOURAGING YOUR CHILD'S SELF-CARE AND SELF-COMPASSION **96**

8.1. The Importance of Self-Care and Self-Compassion **97**

8.2. Developing A Self-Care Plan with Your Child **98**

8.3. Encouraging Self-Compassion in Your Child **99**

8.4. Ventures **100**

CHAPTER 9: MOVING FORWARD WITH YOUR CHILD'S HEALING **111**

9.1. Celebrating Progress with Your Child **111**

9.2. Setting Goals for The Future with Your Child......................**112**

9.3. Planning for Potential Setbacks..**113**

9.4. Ventures **115**

CONCLUSION **124**

Few Words for Rising Stars

Dear Young Readers,

I am excited to introduce you to "The Childhood Trauma Workbook for Kids 9-12," a guide to help you master your past wounds and get healed from PTSD. This book is specially designed for you, with interactive exercises, helpful tips, and fun activities to guide you through the process of healing.

Childhood trauma can be tough to deal with, but with the help of this workbook, you can learn how to cope with your feelings, overcome negative thoughts, and start feeling better. The book will teach you how to use Cognitive Behavioral Therapy (CBT) techniques to challenge negative thoughts, build self-esteem, and manage anxiety.

Through this book, you will learn how to move from surviving to thriving and become the best version of yourself. So, let's start this journey together toward healing and happiness!

Introduction

Childhood trauma can affect anyone, even celebrities, who happen to have it. One such example is Oprah Winfrey, one of the most successful and beloved media personalities in the world. Oprah's traumatic childhood began when she was just nine years old, and her mother sent her to live with her father in Nashville. There, Oprah was subjected to physical and emotional abuse by her father and his family members. She also experienced sexual abuse by several men, including family members, a friend of her mother, and a teenage boy from her neighborhood.

Despite the trauma she endured, Oprah persevered and went on to become one of the most successful and influential women in the world. Through therapy and self-reflection, she was able to confront her past traumas and use her experiences to help others heal. Oprah's story serves as a reminder that childhood trauma does not define a person's future, and with the right tools and support, anyone can overcome their past wounds and thrive.

One famous person who has shared their story of childhood trauma is actor and comedian Tiffany Haddish. In her memoir "The Last Black Unicorn," she writes about growing up in foster care and experiencing neglect and abuse from her mother. Haddish also shares how her traumatic experiences affected her mental health and relationships as an adult, including struggles with PTSD and suicidal thoughts. Despite these challenges, Haddish has found healing through therapy and humor, using her platform to raise awareness about childhood trauma and advocate for better support for foster children.

The effects of childhood trauma can be far-reaching and may affect individuals from any background or age group, regardless of gender, socioeconomic status, or cultural heritage. Childhood trauma can manifest in numerous ways, including but not limited to physical, emotional, or sexual abuse, neglect, or exposure to violence or catastrophic events. The effects of childhood trauma can be far-reaching and long-lasting, affecting a person's mental, emotional, and physical health, as well as their ability to form healthy relationships and achieve their full potential. It is important to recognize the widespread nature of childhood trauma and work towards creating a supportive and healing environment for those affected.

The impact of childhood trauma is multifaceted and distressing, often leaving long-lasting consequences on an individual's well-being. The repercussions of trauma can surface in different forms, such as anxiety, depression, and post-traumatic stress disorder (PTSD). The effects of trauma can be particularly challenging for children, who may struggle with expressing their emotions and seeking help. This is where "The Childhood Trauma Workbook for Kids 9-12 comes in.

This workbook has been designed to help children and their parents understand and cope with the effects of trauma using evidence-based cognitive-behavioral therapy (CBT) techniques. Through a series of engaging and interactive exercises, children will learn how to identify and manage their emotions, develop healthy coping strategies, and build a sense of self-compassion and resilience.

To give a real-life example, consider a child who has experienced physical abuse from a parent. The trauma can lead to the feelings of fear, anxiety, and low self-esteem. The child may struggle to express these emotions and withdraw from social interactions. However, by using the techniques in this workbook, the child can learn how to identify and express their emotions, develop healthy coping mechanisms, and build self-esteem. Through the support of a trusted adult and the exercises in the workbook, the child can begin to heal from their trauma and move towards a healthier, happier life.

Overall, "The Childhood Trauma Workbook for Kids 9-12" is an essential resource for any parent whose child has experienced trauma and is seeking to move beyond surviving to thrive. This workbook empowers children to take control of their healing journey and build a brighter future by providing a secure and compassionate environment for them to explore their emotions and develop healthy coping strategies.

Chapter 1: Understanding Childhood Trauma

Childhood trauma is an emotionally charged and distressing experience that stems from the occurrence of a traumatic event or a series of traumatic events during childhood. The profound effects of trauma can persist long after the experience and can deeply affect a child's emotional, psychological, and physical well-being. The events that cause trauma can take many forms, such as physical, emotional, or sexual abuse, neglect, natural disasters, accidents, or witnessing violence or other harrowing situations. The effects of trauma can vary, depending on the severity of the trauma, the age of the child when the trauma occurred, and the child's support system.

Children who experience trauma may exhibit symptoms such as anxiety, depression, anger, or emotional dysregulation. They may struggle with behavioral problems, sleep disturbances, nightmares, flashbacks, and social difficulties. It's important for parents to understand that children who have experienced trauma need special care and support.

Here's a real-life example of how understanding childhood trauma can make a difference for parents:

Samantha is a mother of two young children. Her eldest, a 7-year-old son, has always been a bit of a challenge. He's easily triggered, prone to outbursts of anger and aggression, and often seems anxious and on edge. Samantha has tried everything she can think of to help her son, from talking to him about his feelings to punishing him when he misbehaves. But nothing seems to work, and she's at her wit's end.

One day, Samantha's friend suggests that her son's behavior might be related to childhood trauma. Samantha is skeptical at first, but she starts to research and learn more about trauma and its effects on children. As she reads about the symptoms of trauma, she realizes that many of them describe her son's behavior. She also begins to understand that her son's outbursts aren't a result of him being "bad" or "difficult" but rather a way of coping with his experiences.

With this new understanding, Samantha approaches her son differently. Instead of punishing him for his behavior, she starts to listen more closely to what he's trying to communicate. She asks him open-ended questions and validates his feelings. She also starts to incorporate more calming activities into their daily routine, like reading together or doing yoga. Slowly but surely, Samantha sees a change in her son's behavior. He's still prone to outbursts, but they're less frequent and less intense. He's also more willing to talk to his mom about what's going on with him.

By taking the time to understand childhood trauma and its effects on her son, Samantha is able to approach parenting in a more empathetic and effective way. She is able to provide her son with the support and resources he needed to work through his trauma and develop healthy coping mechanisms.

1.1. Unraveling The Mystery of Childhood Trauma

Childhood trauma is a complex and often misunderstood phenomenon. Unraveling the mystery of childhood trauma requires an understanding of the different types of trauma that can occur, how trauma affects children and the ways in which children can be helped to overcome the effects of trauma.

The experience of childhood trauma can stem from a range of events, including neglect, physical, emotional, or sexual abuse, sudden or unexpected loss, exposure to violence or natural disasters. The effects of trauma can be both immediate and long-lasting, impacting a child's development, behavior, and relationships with others. Traumatized children may struggle with emotional regulation, exhibit aggressive or impulsive behavior, and have difficulty forming healthy attachments with caregivers or peers.

To unravel the mystery of childhood trauma, parents must first recognize the signs of trauma in their child. These may include nightmares, difficulty sleeping, hyper-vigilance, and intense reactions to reminders of the traumatic event. Once identified, parents can help their child through a variety of interventions, including therapy, support groups, and stress-reducing activities like mindfulness or exercise.

It's important for parents to understand that healing from childhood trauma is a process that takes time and patience. Children may require ongoing support and intervention to overcome the effects of trauma, and there may be setbacks along the way. However, with the right support and resources, children can heal and move forward in a positive direction.

1.2. The Many Faces of Childhood Trauma

Childhood trauma can take many different forms and can have a profound impact on a child's life. It can stem from various sources, such as abuse, neglect, violence, loss of a loved one, and other adverse experiences. Traumatic experiences can manifest in different ways, affecting children's emotional, physical, and cognitive development. Some children may exhibit obvious signs of distress, while others may hide their pain behind a mask of normalcy.

For example, a child who has experienced physical abuse may show signs of physical injury, such as bruises or cuts, but may also exhibit emotional distress, such as anxiety or depression. On the other hand, a child who has experienced neglect may not show any visible signs of trauma but may have difficulties forming relationships or developing a sense of trust.

Similarly, a child who has witnessed domestic violence may exhibit behavioral problems such as aggression, while another child who has experienced sexual abuse may exhibit self-harm behaviors or have difficulties with sexual intimacy later in life. These different faces of childhood trauma make it difficult to identify and address, but it's important for parents to recognize the signs and seek help if necessary.

It's also important to note that childhood trauma can have lifelong effects on a child's life, impacting their mental health, relationships, and future success. Therefore, it's crucial for parents to take childhood trauma seriously and seek professional help if their child has experienced any adverse experiences.

1.3. The Ripple Effects of Trauma

Childhood trauma can have far-reaching effects that extend beyond the individual experiencing it. Like a stone thrown into a pond, the ripple effects of trauma can be felt throughout a person's life, affecting their relationships, mental health, and even physical health. For example, a child who experiences neglect or abuse at a young age may grow up with trust issues and struggle to form healthy relationships in adulthood. They may also develop anxiety or depression, which can lead to physical health problems such as heart disease or chronic pain. The ripple effects of trauma can also impact future generations, as the effects of trauma can be passed down through epigenetic changes in DNA. It's important for parents to understand the far-reaching effects of childhood trauma and to seek appropriate support and treatment for themselves and their children to prevent the ripple effects from spreading further.

1.4. How Trauma Can Lead to PTSD

The effects of childhood trauma can be deep-seated and devastating, with the potential to impair a child's emotional and psychological growth, often leading to the development of post-traumatic stress disorder (PTSD) in adulthood. Traumatic events such as physical or sexual abuse, neglect, natural disasters, or exposure to violence can inundate a child's coping mechanisms and shatter their sense of security. These experiences can leave indelible imprints on a child's brain development, which can significantly heighten their vulnerability to developing PTSD later in life.

When a child experiences trauma, their brain can go into "fight or flight" mode, triggering the release of stress hormones such as adrenaline and cortisol. These hormones can affect the child's brain development, leading to changes in the amygdala, hippocampus, and prefrontal cortex, which are all areas of the brain involved in processing emotions, memory, and stress responses.

Children who experience trauma may also struggle with symptoms such as nightmares, flashbacks, and intrusive thoughts. They may avoid situations or triggers that remind them of the traumatic event and may become easily startled or have a heightened sense of vigilance. These symptoms can impact their daily functioning and lead to difficulties in school, social relationships, and overall well-being.

Examples of childhood trauma that can lead to PTSD include:

o *Physical or sexual abuse*
o *Witnessing domestic violence or other forms of violence*
o *Neglect or emotional abuse*
o *Medical trauma*
o *Natural disasters or other traumatic events*

It's important for parents to recognize the signs of trauma in their children and seek appropriate support and treatment. Early intervention can help mitigate the effects of trauma and reduce the risk of long-term consequences such as PTSD.

Chapter 2: Recognizing Your Child's Trauma Symptoms

As a parent, you are constantly looking out for the well-being of your child. It's important to recognize that trauma can have a deep impact on your child's emotional and mental health. It's natural for children to experience a range of emotions, but if you notice persistent and severe changes in their behavior or mood, it could be a sign of trauma. Your child may exhibit symptoms such as irritability, anger, anxiety, depression, and difficulty sleeping or concentrating. They may also avoid things that remind them of the traumatic event or become easily startled. It's important to understand that trauma can manifest in many different ways and that every child responds differently. By being aware of your child's behavior, you can take steps to support them and help them heal.

2.1. The Hidden Wounds: Common Symptoms of Childhood Trauma in Children

Childhood trauma can have hidden wounds that may not be easily recognized or noticed by parents. It is important for parents to be aware of common symptoms that may indicate their child has experienced trauma.

One common symptom is that the child may seem distant or disconnected from others as if they are in a world of their own. They may withdraw from activities they once enjoyed or show a lack of interest in socializing with friends and family. For example, a child who loves playing soccer may suddenly lose interest and no longer want to participate.

Another symptom is increased anxiety or fearfulness. Children who have experienced trauma may become more anxious and worried about everyday situations, such as going to school or being separated from their parents. They may also have nightmares or flashbacks that are related to the traumatic event they experienced.

Children who have experienced trauma may also exhibit regressive behavior, such as bedwetting or thumb-sucking. They may also become clingier and have separation anxiety. This behavior can be a way for the child to cope with the trauma they have experienced, seeking comfort and reassurance from their parents or caregivers.

Furthermore, some children may become aggressive or act out as a result of their trauma. They may have difficulty controlling their emotions and may become easily irritable or angry. For example, a child who witnessed domestic violence in their home may become aggressive with their siblings or peers.

It is important for parents to recognize these symptoms and seek professional help if they suspect their child has experienced trauma. Childhood trauma can have a lasting impact on a child's mental health, but with proper support and treatment, children can learn to heal and move forward in a positive direction.

2.2. When Trauma Speaks Louder: How Trauma Can Affect Your Child's Thoughts, Feelings, and Behaviors

When your child has experienced trauma, it can affect them in ways that are not always obvious. Trauma can seep into their thoughts, feelings, and behaviors, often making it difficult for them to function in their daily lives. For example, a child who has been in a car accident may feel fearful of riding in a car again, leading to avoidance of any activity that involves being in a car. Similarly, a child who has experienced physical abuse may have difficulty trusting others and may lash out in anger as a means of self-protection.

Trauma can also affect a child's thoughts, leading to negative self-talk and beliefs about themselves and the world around them. They may feel that they are to blame for the trauma they experienced or that they are not worthy of love and care. This can result in low self-esteem and difficulties with forming healthy relationships.

In terms of behaviors, trauma can manifest in a variety of ways. A child may exhibit signs of hyperarousal, such as being easily startled or having difficulty sleeping. They may also engage in risk-taking behaviors, such as substance abuse or dangerous activities, to cope with their trauma. On the other hand, some children may withdraw and isolate themselves from others as a means of self-protection.

It's important to understand that these behaviors and symptoms are not a reflection of your child's character or personality. Rather, they are a response to the trauma they have experienced. With the right support and resources, your child can learn to manage their symptoms and move forward in a healthy and positive way.

2.3. Flashbacks and Triggers: Understanding Triggers and Flashbacks in Children

Triggers and flashbacks are common symptoms of trauma that can have a significant impact on children. Triggers are events or situations that remind a child of their traumatic experience and can cause a range of emotional and physical reactions. These reactions may include panic attacks, flashbacks, nightmares, intense fear, or even physical pain.

Flashbacks, on the other hand, are vivid and distressing memories of a traumatic event that can come back to a child at any time. They can be triggered by sights, sounds, smells, or even feelings that remind them of the traumatic experience. Flashbacks can be incredibly overwhelming and can cause a child to feel like they are reliving the traumatic event.

It is important for parents to understand that triggers and flashbacks are not deliberate actions by their child but rather involuntary responses to trauma. Parents can support their children by learning to recognize their child's triggers and helping them develop coping strategies to manage their emotional and physical reactions.

For example, a child who has experienced a car accident may be triggered by the sound of a car honking or the sight of a car crash on TV. They may experience a flashback of the accident and become overwhelmed with fear and anxiety. As a result, the child may avoid getting into a car or refuse to go to school if they have to pass the location of the accident.

In another example, a child who has experienced physical abuse may be triggered by someone raising their voice or a certain tone of voice. They may have a flashback of the abuse and become extremely anxious or fearful. As a result, the child may struggle to communicate effectively or have difficulty trusting others.

By understanding triggers and flashbacks, parents can help their child feel heard and validated, provide support during times of distress, and help their child develop healthy coping mechanisms to manage these symptoms.

2.4 Ventures

Trauma Symptoms

The "Trauma Symptoms" worksheet is an important tool for kids to identify and understand their own trauma symptoms. By recognizing and naming their symptoms, kids can begin to take control of their experiences and develop coping strategies to manage their emotions. By doing so, children can begin to understand how their trauma symptoms impact their daily lives and relationships.

My Trauma Symptoms

Instructions: Trauma can affect people in different ways. This worksheet is designed to help you identify your own trauma symptoms and how they affect you. Read each statement below and circle the number that best describes how often you experience that symptom. Then, write down how that symptom affects you in your daily life.

I feel anxious or worried even when there's no obvious danger around.

(0) Never

(1) Sometimes

(2) Often

(3) Almost always

How this affects me: _____

I have nightmares or flashbacks about the traumatic event.

(0) Never

(1) Sometimes

(2) Often

(3) Almost always

How this affects me: _____

I feel angry or irritable for no apparent reason.

(0) Never

(1) Sometimes

(2) Often

(3) Almost always

How this affects me: _____

I feel sad or hopeless about the future.

(0) Never

(1) Sometimes

(2) Often

(3) Almost always

How this affects me: _____

I feel numb or disconnected from my emotions.

(0) Never

(1) Sometimes

(2) Often

(3) Almost always

How this affects me: _____

I have trouble sleeping or staying asleep.

(0) Never

(1) Sometimes

(2) Often

(3) Almost always

How this affects me: _____

I feel hyper-vigilant or on edge like something bad might happen.

(0) Never

(1) Sometimes

(2) Often

(3) Almost always

How this affects me: _____

I have physical symptoms like headaches, stomachaches, or a racing heart.

(0) Never

(1) Sometimes

(2) Often

(3) Almost always

How this affects me: _____

I avoid certain people, places, or activities because they remind me of the traumatic event.

(0) Never

(1) Sometimes

(2) Often

(3) Almost always

How this affects me: _____

I feel like I'm not myself or like something inside me has changed.

(0) Never

(1) Sometimes

(2) Often

(3) Almost always

How this affects me: _____

Reflection: Look back over your responses. What patterns or themes do you notice? How do these symptoms affect you in your daily life? Are there any symptoms that you feel you need more help with? Talk to a trusted adult or counselor about getting support for your healing journey.

My Triggers and Flashbacks

For children who have suffered trauma, the "My Triggers and Flashbacks" worksheet serves as a crucial instrument to help them cope with their experiences. Trauma can inflict a long-lasting toll on a child's mental well-being, precipitating debilitating symptoms like anxiety, depression, and post-traumatic stress disorder (PTSD).One of the most challenging aspects of trauma is the unpredictability of triggers and flashbacks, which can cause intense emotional and physical reactions. By using the worksheet, children can learn to identify their triggers and understand how they experience flashbacks. This can help them to feel more in control of their symptoms and develop coping strategies for when they are triggered.

Triggers

Thankful 3's

I feel...

WEEKLY MOOD METER

Out of Control

Angry

Upset

Sad

Worried

Overwhelmed

Annoyed

Calm

Happy

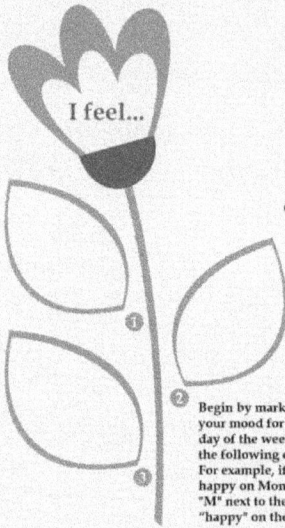

Begin by marking your mood for each day of the week using the following emotions: For example, if you feel happy on Monday, write "M" next to the word "happy" on the Mood Meter.

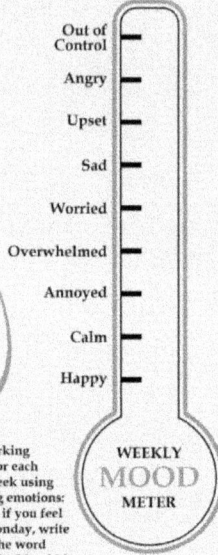

Take a deep breath in for three seconds,

Exhale for six seconds.

Repeat this process by inhaling for two seconds and exhaling for four seconds.

Grounding

Start by identifying five things you can see around you.

1._____
2._____
3._____
4._____
5._____

Then, identify four shapes you can see.

1._____
2._____
3._____
4._____

After that, focus on three things you can touch with your hand.

1._____
2._____
3._____

Next, listen for two sounds you can hear.

1._____
2._____

Finally, identify one emotion that you are feeling.

1._____

My Triggers
and Flashbacks

Instructions: Trauma can cause people to have strong reactions to certain things or situations that remind them of the traumatic event. This worksheet is designed to help you identify your triggers and how you experience flashbacks. Fill in the blanks and discuss your answers with your parent or caregiver.

I.   What are some things or situations that trigger your trauma symptoms? Examples: loud noises, certain smells, being alone, crowded places, specific people or places, etc.

_____

_____

_____

_____

_____

II.   How do you know when you are triggered? What physical sensations, emotions, or thoughts do you experience? Examples: heart racing, sweating, feeling anxious or scared, feeling angry or irritable, having negative thoughts or memories, etc.

_____

_____

_____

_____

_____

III. How do you cope when you are triggered? What strategies help you feel better or calm down? Examples: taking deep breaths, talking to someone, using a stress ball or fidget toy, listening to music, going for a walk, etc.

_____

_____

_____

_____

IV. Have you ever experienced a flashback? What was it like? How did you feel during and after the flashback?

_____

_____

_____

_____

V. How can your parent or caregiver help you when you are triggered or experiencing a flashback? What do you need from them to feel safe and supported?

_____

_____

_____

_____

VI. Talk with your parent or caregiver about your triggers and flashbacks. How can you work together to manage your symptoms and feel more in control? Consider seeking help from a mental health professional if your trauma symptoms are interfering with your daily life. Remember that healing is possible, and you are not alone.

_____

_____

_____

_____

Effective Strategy for Managing Worries: A Step-by-Step Guide

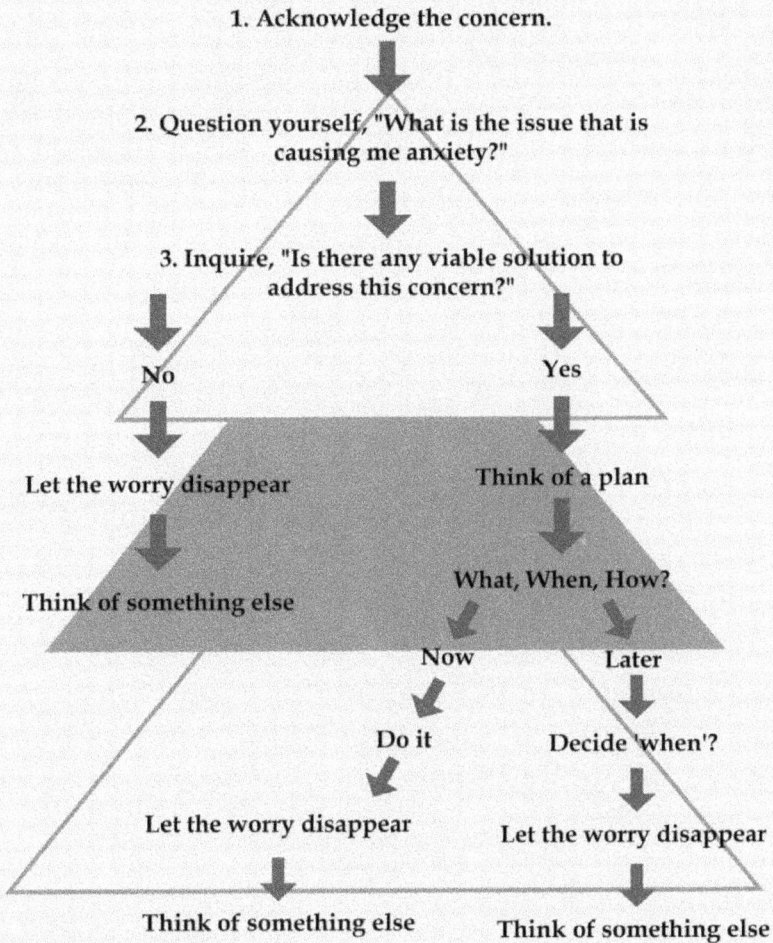

1. Acknowledge the concern.

↓

2. Question yourself, "What is the issue that is causing me anxiety?"

↓

3. Inquire, "Is there any viable solution to address this concern?"

No → **Let the worry disappear** → **Think of something else**

Yes → **Think of a plan** → **What, When, How?**

Now → **Do it** → **Let the worry disappear** → **Think of something else**

Later → **Decide 'when'?** → **Let the worry disappear** → **Think of something else**

Chapter 3: The Role of CBT in Healing Childhood Trauma

CBT (Cognitive Behavioral Therapy) can help children who have experienced trauma by identifying and challenging negative thought patterns and behaviors that may be causing distress. Through therapy sessions, children can learn coping skills, relaxation techniques, and other strategies to manage their symptoms and improve their overall well-being. CBT can be an effective treatment for trauma-related conditions such as PTSD, anxiety, and depression.

3.1. Unlocking The Power of CBT: A Comprehensive Guide

Cognitive Behavioral Therapy (CBT) is a dynamic and evidence-based approach that seeks to tackle maladaptive thoughts, emotions, and behaviors head-on. It is a structured and goal-oriented therapeutic intervention that has demonstrated remarkable efficacy in addressing a diverse array of mental health disorders, including childhood trauma.

CBT is centered around the intricate interplay between thoughts, emotions, and behaviors, and how they can mutually influence each other. The crux of the matter is that negative thoughts and beliefs can engender negative emotions and behaviors. By disrupting these harmful patterns, CBT empowers individuals to cultivate positive thinking patterns and develop constructive coping mechanisms to deal with their traumatic experiences.

Here are some CBT methods that can be helpful in dealing with childhood trauma:

- ✓ **Cognitive Restructuring** involves identifying and challenging negative thoughts and beliefs that an individual may hold about themselves, others, or the world. With the therapist's guidance, they can examine the evidence that supports or contradicts these beliefs and develop more positive and realistic ways of thinking.
- ✓ **Exposure Therapy** is a gradual process that exposes an individual to triggers of anxiety or fear in a controlled environment. This process helps the individual confront their fears and develop new coping strategies.
- ✓ **Relaxation Techniques,** such as progressive muscle relaxation, visualization, and deep breathing are essential for managing anxiety and stress levels. These techniques provide individuals with the tools they need to overcome their traumatic experiences and move with their lives.
- ✓ **Behavioral Activation**: This method involves identifying and scheduling activities that the individual enjoys and finds rewarding. This approach can lead to an upsurge in positive emotions and a decrease in negative emotions. CBT can be helpful for both the children and parents. For children, CBT can provide them with tools and strategies to manage their thoughts and emotions related to childhood trauma. By learning to identify and challenge negative patterns of thinking, they can develop more positive ways of coping with their experiences. For parents, CBT can help them to better understand their child's experiences and provide them with tools and strategies to support their child's recovery. By learning to recognize and address negative patterns of thinking and

behavior in their child, they can help their child to develop more positive ways of coping with their experiences.

3.2. The Healing Power of CBT: A Proven Method for Overcoming Childhood Trauma

Cognitive Behavioral Therapy, an approach that focuses on altering negative thought patterns and behaviors, has proven to be a valuable tool in treating childhood trauma among young people.

Here are some CBT tools and strategies that can help individuals to manage their beliefs and sentiments related to childhood trauma. These tools and strategies are used by therapists but parents can also follow up with these activities.

✓ **Cognitive Restructuring**: A significant aspect of this therapeutic approach is the process of recognizing and confronting pessimistic thoughts and convictions concerning oneself, others, and the world. For example, if an individual believes that they are "unworthy" because of their childhood trauma, a therapist using cognitive restructuring may encourage them to examine the evidence for and against this belief. Furthermore, this technique can aid individuals in cultivating more affirmative and pragmatic views about themselves, like "I am deserving of love and respect, and I am capable of achieving my goals."

Cognitive restructuring is a useful tool for children who have experienced childhood trauma. Here is an example of how it might work:

Let's say a child who has experienced trauma has a belief that "nothing good ever happens to me." This belief may lead to feelings of sadness, hopelessness, and vulnerability, and may even impact the child's behavior and relationships with others. A therapist using cognitive restructuring might guide the child through the following steps:

Identify the negative belief: The therapist might ask the child to talk about the thoughts and feelings they have when they think "nothing good ever happens to me."

Challenge the negative belief: The therapist might help the child to explore the evidence for and against this belief. They might ask questions like "Can you think of a time when something good did happen to you?" or "Do you think it's fair to say that absolutely nothing good ever happens to you?"

Develop a more positive and realistic belief: The therapist might work with the child to develop a more positive and realistic belief that they can use instead of the negative one. For example, they might help the child to come up with a statement like "Sometimes things don't go the way I want them to, but good things do happen to me sometimes."

Practice the new belief: The therapist might encourage the child to practice using the new belief in everyday situations. For example, they might ask the child to repeat the new belief to themselves when they start to feel sad or hopeless.

✓ **Thought-Stopping**: This tool involves interrupting negative or intrusive thoughts by saying "stop" or visualizing a stop sign. The individual then replaces the negative thought with a positive one. For example, if an individual is experiencing intrusive thoughts related to their trauma, they may say "stop" and replace the thought with a positive affirmation such as "I am safe and in control."

Thought-stopping is a useful technique for children who may be experiencing intrusive or negative thoughts related to their childhood trauma. Here is an example of how it might work:

Let's say a child who has experienced trauma has a thought that "I'm not safe" whenever they hear a loud noise. This thought may lead to feelings of anxiety, fear, and helplessness. A therapist using thought-stopping might guide the child through the following steps:

Identify the negative thought: *The therapist might ask the child to talk about the thoughts and feelings they have when they hear a loud noise.*

Introduce the thought-stopping technique: *The therapist might explain to the child that they can use a technique called thought-stopping to interrupt the negative thought.*

Practice the technique: *The therapist might ask the child to imagine hearing a loud noise and then saying "stop" out loud or visualizing a stop sign. The child can then replace the negative thought with a positive one, such as "I am safe."*

Reinforce the technique: *The therapist might encourage the child to practice using the thought-stopping technique in everyday situations. For example, they might ask the child to use the technique whenever they hear a loud noise at home or at school.*

By utilizing thought-stopping techniques, children can acquire the ability to disrupt negative thought patterns and replace them with more constructive and optimistic ones. This can help them to feel more in control and reduce feelings of anxiety, fear, and helplessness. It's important to note that thought-stopping should be guided by a trained therapist who can help the child to practice the technique in a safe and supportive environment.

✓ **Grounding Techniques**: These techniques involve focusing on the present moment to manage feelings of anxiety or dissociation. For example, an individual may focus on their surroundings, describing what they see, hear, smell, and feel in the moment. They may also use mindfulness techniques such as deep breathing to help them stay present.

Grounding techniques are helpful for children who may be feeling overwhelmed or dissociated due to their childhood trauma. Here is an example of how it might work:

Let's say a child who has experienced trauma is feeling overwhelmed and disconnected from their surroundings. A therapist using grounding techniques might guide the child through the following steps:

Identify the feeling: *The therapist might ask the child to describe the sensations they are experiencing in their body and how they are feeling emotionally.*

Introduce the grounding technique: *The therapist might explain to the child that they can use a technique called grounding to help them feel more connected to their surroundings.*

Practice the technique: *The therapist might ask the child to focus on their five senses, such as looking around the room and describing what they see, listening to the sounds in the room and describing what they hear, or holding an object and describing how it feels. The child can also focus on their breathing, taking deep breaths and counting to five on each inhale and exhale.*

Reinforce the technique: The therapist might encourage the child to practice using the grounding technique in everyday situations. For example, they might ask the child to use the technique when they start to feel overwhelmed at school or at home.

Through grounding techniques, children can learn to connect with their surroundings and feel more in control of their thoughts and emotions. This can help them to feel more present and reduce feelings of dissociation or overwhelm. It's important to note that grounding techniques should be guided by a trained therapist who can help the child to practice the technique in a safe and supportive environment.

✓ **Imagery Rehearsal Therapy**: This tool involves using visualization techniques to rehearse positive experiences or coping strategies. For example, an individual may visualize themselves successfully managing a triggering situation or feeling confident and empowered.

Imagery Rehearsal Therapy (IRT) is a technique that is commonly used to help children who have experienced childhood trauma to overcome nightmares or disturbing dreams. Here is an example of how it might work:

Identify the problematic dream: The therapist might ask the child to describe the nightmare or disturbing dream that they have been experiencing. They may also ask the child to describe how they feel during and after the dream.

Create a new, positive dream: The therapist will work with the child to create a new dream that replaces the old, negative dream. The new dream should be positive, empowering, and should help the child to feel safe and in control.

Practice the new dream: The child will be encouraged to practice the new dream several times a day, using vivid imagery and positive self-talk. The therapist may also use relaxation techniques, such as progressive muscle relaxation or deep breathing to help the child relax and feel comfortable while they practice the new dream.

Reinforce the new dream: The therapist will encourage the child to continue practicing the new dream, and may also ask them to keep a dream journal to track their progress. Over time, the new dream will replace the old, negative dream, and the child will experience fewer nightmares or disturbing dreams.

Through Imagery Rehearsal Therapy, children can learn to reprogram their thoughts and feelings related to traumatic experiences and replace them with positive, empowering thoughts and feelings. It's important to note that IRT should be guided by a trained therapist who can help the child to create and practice the new dream in a safe and supportive environment.

- ✓ **Behavioral Activation**: This tool involves scheduling and engaging in enjoyable activities as a way to increase positive emotions and reduce negative ones. For example, an individual may schedule time to engage in hobbies, spend time with loved ones, or engage in physical exercise.

Behavioral Activation is a technique that can be used to help children who have experienced childhood trauma to overcome depression or other negative emotions. Here is an example of how it might work:

Identify the child's preferred activities: The therapist will work with the child to identify activities that the child enjoys and finds meaningful.

These may include hobbies, sports, social activities, or other forms of recreation.

Schedule regular activities: *The therapist will help the child to schedule these activities on a regular basis, such as once a week or every other day. This will help the child to build a sense of structure and routine into their life.*

Monitor progress: *The therapist will encourage the child to track their progress in completing the scheduled activities. This will help the child to see how their efforts are making a positive difference in their life.*

Reinforce positive behavior: *The therapist will provide positive reinforcement to the child for completing the scheduled activities, such as praise or rewards. This will help the child to feel motivated and encouraged to continue with the behavioral activation program.*

Through Behavioral Activation, children can learn to engage in positive activities that promote a sense of well-being and help to reduce negative emotions such as depression, anxiety, or helplessness. It's important to note that Behavioral Activation should be guided by a trained therapist who can help the child to schedule and complete activities in a safe and supportive environment.

These are just a few examples of the tools and strategies that CBT can offer for managing thoughts and emotions related to childhood trauma. It is crucial to note that the selection of tools and approaches employed in therapy may differ depending on the individual's particular needs and experiences. Moreover, it is advisable to conduct such interventions under the supervision of a competent therapist.

Helping Kids Understand Their Thoughts, Feelings, and Actions: Using the CBT Model

What occurred or took place?

What were you thinking at that time?

How did it make you feel?

What physical sensations were you experiencing?

What actions did you take or how did you behave in response to the situation?

3.3. The ABCs of Healing: How CBT's ABC Model Helps Your Child Identify and Change Negative Thought Patterns

CBT's ABC model is a powerful tool for helping children identify and change negative thought patterns. Here is a breakdown of how it works:

A - Activating Event: *The activating event is the trigger that sets off a chain reaction of negative thoughts, feelings, and behaviors. For example, a child might experience an activating event when they are teased by a classmate.*

B - Beliefs: *The beliefs are the negative thoughts that arise in response to the activating event. These thoughts are often automatic and can be irrational or unhelpful. For example, the child might believe "I am worthless" or "Nobody likes me."*

C - Consequences: *The consequences are the emotional and behavioral reactions that follow from the views. For example, the child might feel sad, anxious, or angry and may withdraw from social situations or lash out at others.*

CBT helps children identify and challenge their negative beliefs, leading to more positive consequences. Here are some examples of how this might work:

- o **Challenge negative beliefs**: If a child believes "I am worthless," a therapist might help them explore the evidence for and against this belief. They might ask the child to think of times when they felt proud of themselves or when others showed them kindness, helping to build a more balanced and realistic view of themselves.

- o **Replace negative thoughts**: Once a child has identified a negative thought pattern, a therapist can help them come up with more positive and helpful thoughts to replace it. For example, instead of thinking, "Nobody likes me," a child might learn to reframe their thoughts as "Some people don't like me, but there are plenty of people who do."
- o **Behavioral experiments**: CBT also encourages children to test their negative beliefs in the real world. For example, a child who believes "I can't do anything right" might be asked to try a new activity and see how it goes. If they succeed, it can help to challenge their negative beliefs and build confidence.

By using the ABC model and other CBT techniques, therapists can help children overcome their negative thought patterns and build more positive coping strategies.

3.4. Ventures

My ABCs

The "My ABCs" worksheet can help kids by providing a structured and organized approach to identifying and understanding their thoughts, feelings, and behaviors in response to a triggering situation. By breaking down the situation into its various components (the activating event, beliefs, and consequences), children can gain insight into their own thinking patterns and how these patterns may be contributing to their negative feelings and behaviors. With this understanding, children can then work on changing their negative thought patterns and developing more positive coping strategies.

My ABCs

Instructions: The ABC model is a tool that can help you understand how your thoughts, feelings, and behaviors are connected. Use this worksheet to practice using the ABC model to identify your own thoughts, feelings, and behaviors in response to a triggering situation. Fill in the blanks and think about how you can use this information to manage your emotions.

A = Activating Event: What happened to trigger your emotions?

B = Beliefs: What thoughts or beliefs do you have about the activating event?

C = Consequences: What are the feelings and behaviors that result from your thoughts and beliefs?

Example:

A = Activating Event: I got a bad grade on my math test.

B = Beliefs: I'm never going to be good at math. My teacher probably thinks I'm stupid.

C = Consequences: I feel sad and disappointed in myself. I don't want to do my homework, and I don't want to go to math class.

Now it's your turn:

A = Activating Event:

_____

B = Beliefs:

_____

C = Consequences:

_____

Reflection: *How did using the ABC model help you understand your thoughts, feelings, and behaviors? What can you do to challenge negative thoughts or beliefs and change the consequences? Remember that it's okay to make mistakes or have difficult emotions and that you can always ask for help from a trusted adult or mental health professional if you need it.*

Replacing Negative Thoughts

The "Replacing Negative Thoughts" worksheet is a valuable tool in assisting children to recognize their pessimistic thoughts and substitute them with more constructive and pragmatic ones. This worksheet provides children with practical techniques to change their thought patterns and promote positive thinking.

Replacing Negative Thoughts

Instructions for parents: Negative thoughts can be difficult for kids to manage and can impact their emotions and behavior. This worksheet can help your child practice identifying and replacing negative thoughts with more positive and realistic ones. Use this worksheet with your child and guide them through the steps.

Identify the negative thought: Ask your child to identify a negative thought they have been having recently.

Negative thoughts identified by the child:

_____

_____

_____

_____

Challenge the negative thought: Ask your child if the negative thought is true or helpful. Ask them to think about evidence that supports or contradicts the negative thought.

Questions for parents to guide their child:

- Is the negative thought true?
- Is it helpful?
- What evidence do you have to support or contradict the negative thought?
- Evidence identified by a child:

_____

_____

_____

_____

Replace the negative thought: Help your child come up with a more positive and realistic thought to replace the negative one.

Questions for parents to guide their child:

- What would be a more positive and realistic thought to replace the negative one?
- How can you reframe the situation in a more positive light?
- Positive thoughts identified by a child:

_____

_____

_____

_____

_____

_____

Practice the positive thought: Encourage your child to repeat the positive thought to themselves, write it down, or visualize it in their mind. Ask them how it makes them feel.

Questions for parents to guide their child:

- How can you practice positive thought?
- How does the positive thought make you feel?
- Practice and feelings described by a child:

_____

_____

_____

_____

_____

_____

Reflection: *Talk to your child about how replacing negative thoughts with positive ones can help them feel better and manage their emotions. Encourage them to continue using this worksheet to identify and replace negative thoughts. Remember to offer support and help your child seek professional help if needed.*

Chapter 4: Helping Your Child Challenge Negative Thoughts and Beliefs

Cognitive-behavioral therapy (CBT) is an evidence-based approach that helps individuals to confront negative thinking patterns and beliefs that may be hindering their emotional well-being or causing negative behaviors. The goal of CBT is to equip individuals with the skills and tools necessary to challenge and replace negative thoughts with positive and realistic ones, ultimately helping them to lead a more fulfilling life.

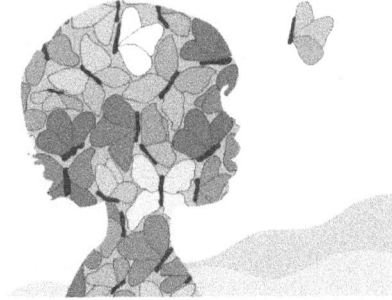

4.1. Uncovering The Roots of Negative Thoughts and Beliefs in Your Child

Uncovering the roots of negative thoughts and beliefs in your child is an essential step in helping them challenge and overcome them.

Here are some points to help explain how parents can uncover the roots of negative thoughts and beliefs in their children:

> o **Pay attention to your child's behavior**: *Negative thoughts and beliefs can manifest in a child's behavior. If your child is frequently upset or anxious, it may be an indication of underlying negative thoughts or beliefs.*
>
> o **Listen to your child:** *Encourage your child to express their thoughts and feelings. Listen attentively and empathetically without judgment, criticism or interruption. Make them feel comfortable and safe.*

- o **Observe their communication style:** *Notice how your child communicates with others, including tone of voice and body language. This can be an indication of how they feel about themselves and their beliefs.*
- o **Look for patterns:** *Negative thoughts and beliefs can develop from specific events or situations. Observe your child's behavior and thoughts in different scenarios to identify any patterns or triggers.*
- o **Identify any past traumatic experiences:** *Childhood trauma can lead to negative thoughts and beliefs. If your child has experienced any traumatic events, it may be impacting their thoughts and beliefs. Seek professional help if needed.*
- o **Consider family dynamics:** *Negative thoughts and beliefs can also stem from family dynamics. If there are conflicts or issues within the family, they can impact a child's self-esteem and beliefs about themselves.*

4.2. Weighing the Evidence: Challenging Negative Thoughts and Beliefs with Facts

Weighing the evidence involves examining negative thoughts and beliefs and challenging them with factual evidence. The transformative process of CBT can empower children to develop a more optimistic and affirmative perspective on themselves and their environment. Here are some examples of how parents can help their children challenge negative thoughts and beliefs with facts:

Negative Thought: "I am a failure because I didn't get an A on my test."

Challenging with Facts: Encourage your child to look at the evidence objectively. Did they study hard for the test? Did they do their best? If they can answer yes to these questions, then getting a B or a C does not make them a failure.

Negative Thought: "No one likes me."

Challenging with Facts: Ask your child to identify people in their life who have shown them kindness or friendship. Encourage them to think about the positive interactions they have had with others and remind them that one negative experience does not define their worth or likeability.

Negative Thought: "I'm never going to be good at anything."

Challenging with Facts: Help your child to identify the areas in which they have shown improvement or success in the past. Encourage them to set small achievable goals and work towards them. This will help them build confidence and recognize their abilities.

By challenging negative thoughts and beliefs with facts, children can begin to see situations and themselves in a more positive light.

4.3. Empowering Your Child: Techniques to Replace Negative Thoughts with Positive Ones

A crucial step in helping children overcome negative beliefs that may have resulted from childhood trauma is to empower them to replace negative thoughts with positive ones. Here are some techniques parents can use to help their child:

- *Positive Affirmations: Encourage your child to create a list of positive statements about themselves, such as "I am strong" or "I am capable." These affirmations can be repeated daily to reinforce positive beliefs.*

- **Gratitude Practice:** *Help your child focus on the positive aspects of their life by practicing gratitude. Encourage them to list things they are grateful for each day, such as a good friend or a fun activity they participated in.*

- **Visualization:** *Encourage your child to visualize positive outcomes to situations that have previously triggered negative thoughts. For example, if your child gets anxious before a test, have them visualize themselves feeling calm and confident during the test.*

- *Cognitive Restructuring: Help your child reframe negative thoughts by encouraging them to look for evidence that contradicts their negative beliefs. For example, if they believe they are "stupid," have them list examples of times they have succeeded academically or in other areas.*

- *Role-Playing: Practice situations with your child where they can replace negative thoughts with positive ones. For example, if your child gets nervous before a presentation, have them practice thinking positive thoughts, such as "I am well-prepared" or "I am a good speaker."*

By practicing these techniques regularly, parents can help their child replace negative thoughts with positive ones; building their self-esteem and helping them overcome negative beliefs that may have developed due to childhood trauma.

4.4. Ventures

Evidence for and Against

The worksheet "Evidence for and Against" is a powerful tool that empowers children to challenge and overcome their negative thoughts and beliefs. With a structured way to evaluate their thoughts, children can objectively identify evidence that supports or undermines their negative beliefs. By doing so, they can replace them with positive and accurate ones, developing a resilient mindset that can withstand the effects of childhood trauma. This worksheet enables children to take control of their thoughts and emotions, helping them to become stronger and more confident individuals.

Evidence for and Against

Instructions for parents: Negative thoughts and beliefs can be challenging for kids to manage and can impact their emotions and behavior. This worksheet can help your child practice identifying evidence for and against negative thoughts and beliefs they may have about themselves, others, or the world. Use this worksheet with your child and guide them through the steps.

Identify the negative thought or belief: Ask your child to identify a negative thought or belief they may have about themselves, others, or the world.

Negative thought/belief identified by a child:

_____

_____

_____

List evidence for the negative thought/belief: Ask your child to think of evidence that supports the negative thought or belief.

Questions for parents to guide their child:

- What evidence do you have to support the negative thought or belief?
- Have you experienced situations that confirm negative thought or belief?
- Evidence for the negative thought/belief identified by child:

_____

_____

_____

List evidence against the negative thought/belief: Ask your child to think of evidence that contradicts the negative thought or belief.

Questions for parents to guide their child:

- Is there evidence that contradicts the negative thought or belief?
- Have you experienced situations that contradict the negative thought or belief?
- Evidence against the negative thought/belief identified by a child:

_____

_____

_____

Evaluate the evidence: Ask your child to evaluate the evidence for and against the negative thought or belief.

Questions for parents to guide their child:

- Which evidence is stronger?
- Does the evidence support or contradict the negative thought or belief?
- Evaluation of evidence by a child:

_____

_____

Replace the negative thought/belief: Help your child come up with a more positive and realistic thought or belief to replace the negative one.

Questions for parents to guide their child:

- What would be a more positive and realistic thought or belief to replace the negative one?
- How can you reframe the situation in a more positive light?
- Positive thought/belief identified by a child:

_____

_____

Practice the positive thought/belief: Encourage your child to repeat the positive thought/belief to themselves, write it down, or visualize it in their mind. Ask them how it makes them feel.

Questions for parents to guide their child:

- How can you practice the positive thought/belief?
- How does the positive thought/belief make you feel?
- Practice and feelings described by child:

_____

_____

_____

Reflection: Empower your child by discussing how identifying evidence for and against negative thoughts can help them view situations more objectively. Encourage them to continue using this worksheet to challenge negative thoughts and beliefs. Remember to offer your unwavering support and help your child seek professional assistance if necessary.

Positive Affirmations

"Positive Affirmations" worksheet can help kids create statements that challenge their negative thoughts and beliefs. By replacing negative self-talk with positive affirmations, children can improve their self-esteem and confidence. This worksheet encourages children to reflect on their positive qualities and create statements that reflect them. Examples of positive affirmations may include "I am capable," "I am strong," or "I am worthy of love and respect." By repeating these positive affirmations, children can replace negative thoughts with positive ones, and feel more empowered and confident in themselves.

Positive Affirmations

Instructions: In the space provided, write down positive affirmations that challenge negative thoughts and beliefs that you may have about yourself. Try to make these affirmations specific and meaningful to you.

1. _____

2. _____

3. _____

4. _____

5. _____

6. _____

7. _____

8. _____

9. _____

10. _____

Let's help your kids connect their Thoughts, feelings and actions through this activity.

Bonus: *Choose one or two affirmations from your list and repeat them to yourself each day for a week. Notice how you feel and any changes in your thoughts or behaviors.*

MAPPING YOUR THOUGHTS, FEELINGS, AND ACTIONS

Steps:

Identify triggers that cause a certain reaction in you.

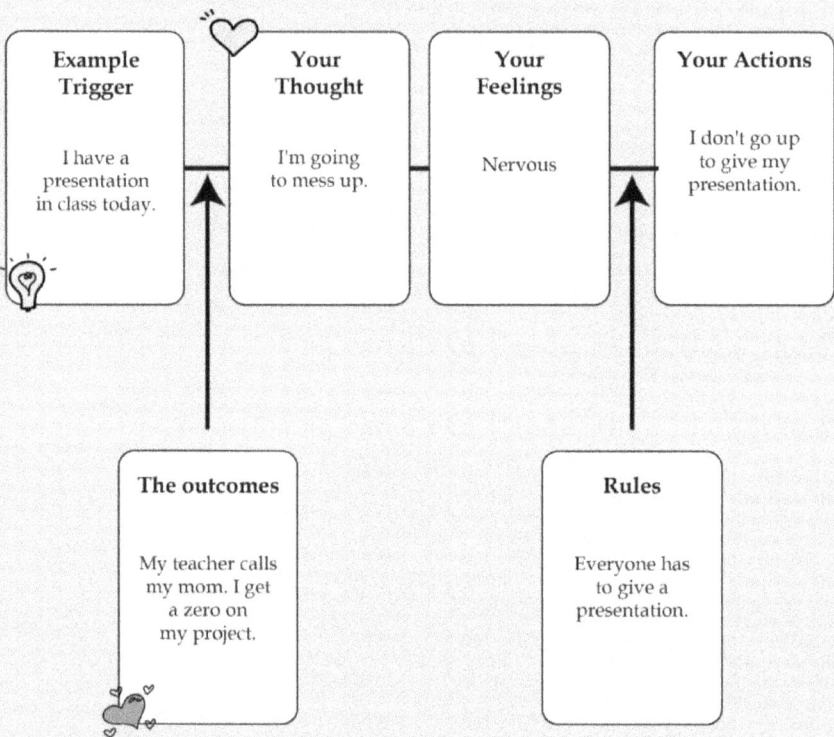

Example Trigger	Your Thought	Your Feelings	Your Actions
I have a presentation in class today.	I'm going to mess up.	Nervous	I don't go up to give my presentation.

The outcomes

My teacher calls my mom. I get a zero on my project.

Rules

Everyone has to give a presentation.

Chapter 5: Supporting Your Child's Coping Strategies for Managing Trauma Symptoms

Supporting your child's coping strategies for managing trauma symptoms involves providing a safe and nurturing environment, helping your child to identify and express their feelings, teaching them relaxation techniques, and encouraging healthy coping mechanisms such as exercise and creative outlets Collaborating with your child's healthcare provider to create a personalized treatment plan that caters to their specific needs is crucial.

5.1. Breathing Exercises

Breathing exercises can be an effective tool to assist your child in coping with trauma symptoms. These exercises can assist your child in regulating their emotions, decreasing their anxiety, and managing their stress levels. Some examples of easy breathing techniques are deep breathing, belly breathing, and box breathing.

Deep Breathing involves inhaling through the nose, filling the lungs with air, and exhaling slowly through the mouth to completely empty the lungs.

Belly Breathing involves placing one hand on the chest and the other on the belly, inhaling deeply through the nose while feeling the belly rise, and then exhaling slowly through the mouth while feeling the belly fall.

> **Box Breathing** *where individuals inhale slowly for four counts, hold their breath for four counts, exhale slowly for four counts, and hold their breath for four counts before starting the cycle again.*

You can motivate your child to practice these breathing exercises in a peaceful and quiet environment at home and incorporate them into their everyday routine. You can also suggest them to utilize these exercises when they feel overwhelmed or anxious or before participating in activities that may trigger their trauma symptoms. By teaching your child these coping strategies and giving them the resources to manage their trauma symptoms, you can assist them in feeling more in control of their emotions and enhance their overall well-being.

5.2. Mindfulness Practices

Mindfulness practices can be a helpful approach to supporting children coping with trauma symptoms. Practicing mindfulness involves being fully present in the moment without any judgment or distractions, which can help children increase their self-awareness and regulate their thoughts and emotions effectively, preventing them from becoming overwhelmed.

Various techniques can be employed to encourage mindfulness in children, including body scans, mindful breathing, mindful movement, mindful eating, guided meditation, and art therapy. A body scan involves focusing on each body part to identify any physical sensations or tension, which helps release stress and promote relaxation. Mindful breathing is about taking slow and deep breaths, focusing on the sensation of breathing to calm the nervous system and reduce anxiety.

Mindful movement, such as yoga or tai chi is a gentle form of exercise that encourages children to be more aware of their body and release tension. Engaging in mindful eating requires an individual to focus on the present moment, including the sensory details of the food being consumed, such as its taste, texture, and aroma. This practice has the potential to induce a feeling of tranquility and ease.

Guided meditation requires listening to a guide who encourages children to focus on their breath, body sensations, or visualizations. This can help them feel more relaxed and focused. Art therapy is another technique that uses creative expression to help children express their thoughts and emotions in a safe and non-judgmental environment. Art can also be used as a mindfulness practice, where children can focus on the present moment and engage in creating art, which can help reduce anxiety and improve mood.

Parents can support their child's mindfulness practice by encouraging them to practice these techniques regularly and creating a safe and comfortable space for them to do so. Parents can also participate in the practice with their child to model the behavior and emphasize the importance of self-care.

5.3. Grounding Techniques

Grounding techniques can be a helpful coping strategy for children who have experienced trauma. These techniques can help children feel more present at the moment and reduce the severity of their trauma symptoms. Here are some methods of grounding techniques that can support your child's coping strategies for managing trauma symptoms:

Five Senses Grounding: Ask your child to focus on each of their senses (sight, sound, touch, smell, taste) and name five things they notice for each sense. This helps them to be present at the moment and focused on the present.

Breathing Grounding: Ask your child to take deep breaths and focus on their breath as they inhale and exhale. You can also ask them to count their breaths as they take them.

Progressive Muscle Relaxation: You can help your child relax and be more present in the moment by guiding them through tensing and releasing each muscle group in their body, starting from their toes and moving up to their head.

Mindful Walking: Encourage your child to take a slow, mindful walk and focus on the physical sensations of walking, such as the feeling of their feet touching the ground.

Positive Self-Talk: Encouraging your child to engage in positive self-talk can be helpful in managing their emotions during difficult moments. You can assist your child in creating positive affirmations that they can repeat to themselves when they feel stressed or anxious. Examples of affirmations include phrases such as "I am safe," "I am strong," or "I can overcome this." By repeating these positive statements, your child can help to shift their mindset and feel more in control of their emotions. It is essential to create affirmations that resonate with your child's experiences and feelings, as they will be most effective in promoting a positive mindset.

It is important to note that different grounding techniques may work better for different children, and it may take some experimentation to find the most effective techniques for your child. Encourage your child to practice these techniques regularly, even when they are not experiencing trauma symptoms, to help build their resilience and coping skills.

5.4. Self-Soothing Strategies

Self-soothing strategies are techniques that can help children calm down and manage their emotions in a healthy way. Here are some examples of self-soothing strategies that can be helpful for children who have experienced trauma:

> *Visualization:* Encourage your child to imagine a peaceful scene or a happy memory. This can help them feel more positive emotions and reduce stress.
>
> *Sensory activities*: Provide your child with items that have a soothing sensory quality, such as a soft blanket or a stress ball. These items can help your child feel more grounded and secure.
>
> *Mindful coloring or drawing*: Provide your child with paper and coloring or drawing materials and encourage them to focus on the present moment as they create. This can help them feel calmer and more centered.

Finding the most effective self-soothing strategies for your child requires individualized attention and experimentation. Additionally, it's important to provide opportunities for your child to practice these strategies regularly, even when they are not feeling particularly stressed or overwhelmed so that they become a natural part of their coping skills toolbox.

5.5. Ventures

My Grounding Techniques

"My Grounding Techniques" worksheet helps kids identify and practice various techniques that can help them feel calm and present. This worksheet is crucial as it helps children in managing their trauma

symptoms and provides a sense of control over their emotions. It allows children to explore different grounding techniques that work best for them and create a personalized toolkit to cope with trauma triggers. Overall, this worksheet promotes self-awareness and self-regulation in children, leading to improved emotional well-being.

My Grounding Techniques

Instructions: Grounding techniques can help you feel more present and calm when you are feeling overwhelmed or anxious. This worksheet is designed to help you identify and practice different grounding techniques that work for you. Fill in the blanks and practice each technique until you find what works best for you.

Name three things you can see around you:

_____

_____

_____

Name three things you can hear around you:

_____

_____

_____

Name three things you can touch around you:

_____

_____

_____

Take ten deep breaths; counting to 5 on the inhale and five on the exhale:

_____

_____

_____

Use a grounding object, such as a stress ball or fidget toy, and focus on its texture and how it feels in your hands:

_____

_____

_____

_____

Go for a walk and focus on your surroundings, such as the feel of your feet on the ground or the sounds of nature; jot it down:

_____

_____

_____

_____

Use positive self-talk to remind yourself that you are safe and capable of managing your emotions. Now write three positive lines:

_____

_____

_____

_____

Draw or color a picture that makes you feel happy or calm

Wrap yourself in a cozy blanket or hug a stuffed animal; describe your feelings:

_____

_____

_____

Listen to calming music or sounds, such as nature sounds or white noise. Describe how it feels:

_____

_____

_____

Tips:

Take a warm bath or shower, and use scented soap or bath bombs.

Use aromatherapy, such as essential oils or a scented candle.

Have a favorite snack or drink, such as hot cocoa or popcorn.

Write in a journal

Drawing pictures is a helpful way to cope with difficult or unexpected situations that can trigger various emotions. Today, you can use this technique to express and process your current feelings by creating a picture that represents them.

DATE: _____

_____

_____

_____

_____

_____

_____

_____

_____

_____

_____

_____

_____

Instructions: Roll the dice and perform the activities accordingly

Dice	Category			
⚀ (1)	Affirmation	"I am safe"	"I am brave"	"I can handle this situation"
⚁ (2)	Support	Identify someone at school who provides you with support.	Name a friend who provides you with support.	Identify someone at home who provides you with support.
⚂ (3)	Moving	Do wall push-ups.	Do jumping jacks.	Dance to your favorite music.
⚃ (4)	Breathing	Place your hand over your heart.	Do the butterfly technique.	Blow bubbles.
⚄ (5)	Stretching	Do the kite pose. Do the chair pose.	Bring your hands to your heart. Do the frog pose.	Do the triangle pose. Do the warrior pose.
⚅ (6)	Grounding	Identify three things you can hear and two things you can smell.	Identify three green things, two blue things, and one red thing in the room.	Embrace yourself with a hug and state the current day, date, and your location.

Meditation is good for you.

Start by setting a timer for 10 minutes.

Sit in a comfortable position and close your eyes.

Bring your attention to your breathing.

Inhale slowly through your nose and focus on the sound of your breath.

Exhale through your nose.

If your mind wanders, gently redirect your attention back to your breath.

When the timer goes off, slowly open your eyes.

Journal daily to record your meditation experience and how it makes you feel.

It may be tough at first, but don't give up! With consistent practice, you'll be able to meditate like Yoda in no time.

Color Yoda!

Reflection: Practice each grounding technique and pay attention to how it makes you feel. Which techniques work best for you? Make a list of your favorite grounding techniques and keep them with you when you need them. Remember that grounding techniques are a tool to help you manage your emotions, and it's okay to ask for help from a trusted adult or mental health professional if you need it.

Chapter 6: Supporting Your Child in Overcoming Fear and Avoidance

Supporting your child in overcoming fear and avoidance involves providing a safe and supportive environment for them to express their fears and anxieties. Encourage your child to face their fears in a gradual and supportive way rather than avoiding them altogether. Assist them in acquiring coping techniques like belly breathing, present moment awareness, and optimistic self-dialogue. It's also essential to seek professional help if your child's fear and avoidance are interfering with their daily life or causing significant distress.

6.1. Understanding Avoidance Behaviors in Children

Avoidance behaviors in children are common, particularly when they experience fear or anxiety. Here are some examples of avoidance behaviors that children may display:

- o ***Refusal to attend a school or social events:*** *A child may avoid going to school or social events because they fear being in unfamiliar situations or interacting with others.*
- o ***Avoidance of specific activities or tasks***: *Children may avoid certain activities or tasks that they perceive as challenging or difficult, such as public speaking or participating in sports.*
- o ***Repeatedly seeking reassurance***: *A child may seek reassurance from parents or caregivers repeatedly to reduce their anxiety, such as asking if a door is locked multiple times.*

> ○ ***Physical symptoms***: *Some children may display physical symptoms such as headaches, stomach aches, or feeling sick as a way to avoid certain situations or tasks.*
>
> ○ ***Procrastination:*** *Children may procrastinate or delay starting a task or project that causes them anxiety, such as studying for a test or completing a school project.*

It's important to understand that avoidance behaviors can worsen anxiety and limit a child's ability to engage in activities that are important for their growth and development. Parents and caregivers can help children overcome avoidance behaviors by providing support and teaching them coping skills to manage their fears and anxieties.

6.2. Gradual Exposure to Feared Situations

Gradual exposure is a common behavioral technique used to help children overcome their fears and avoidance behaviors. It involves gradually exposing the child to the feared situation or object in a controlled and supportive environment, allowing the child to gradually become more comfortable and less anxious.

The process typically involves several steps, starting with exposure to less threatening stimuli and progressing to more challenging situations over time. For example, a child who is afraid of dogs may begin by looking at pictures of dogs, then watching videos of dogs, followed by interacting with a calm and friendly dog on a leash, and eventually being around an unleashed dog.

The key to successful gradual exposure is to proceed at the child's pace, allowing them to control the intensity of the exposure and to take breaks as needed. It's also important to provide positive reinforcement and encouragement along the way, acknowledging the child's efforts and progress.

Through repeated exposure to the feared situation or object, the child's anxiety and avoidance behaviors can gradually decrease, allowing them to feel more confident and in control. Gradual exposure can be a highly effective technique for helping children overcome their fears and regain their ability to participate in activities and experiences they enjoy.

6.3. Practicing Relaxation Techniques During Exposure

Using relaxation techniques in conjunction with exposure therapy can be a valuable method for helping children overcome fear and avoidance. When a child encounters a situation that triggers fear, it can lead to a stress response in the body, causing feelings of anxiety and tension. However, parents can teach relaxation techniques to their children to help them manage these emotions and deal with the situation in a calmer and controlled manner.

Relaxation techniques that are effective during exposure therapy include deep breathing, progressive muscle relaxation, and visualization. Deep breathing entails inhaling deeply through the nose and exhaling slowly through the mouth, focusing on each breath to promote relaxation. Progressive muscle relaxation is a technique that involves sequentially tensing and relaxing various muscle groups, like the limbs, in order to relieve tension and encourage calmness. Visualization entails visualizing a peaceful and calm scene, such as a beach or forest, to decrease anxiety and promote relaxation.

By practicing these relaxation techniques during exposure therapy, children can learn to manage their anxiety and build confidence in their ability to handle difficult situations. Eventually, these techniques can become an integral part of their coping strategies, enabling them to navigate stressful situations with greater ease and resilience

6.4. Ventures

Courageous Steps: Facing Your Fears with CBT

The "Courageous Steps: Facing Your Fears with CBT" worksheet is an important tool for children who are struggling with fears and anxieties. It provides a structured approach for identifying and understanding their fears, challenging negative thoughts, setting goals and actions, and reinforcing positive behaviors. By using this worksheet, children can develop the skills and confidence to face their fears and improve their mental health and well-being.

Courageous Steps: Facing Your Fears with CBT

Instructions:

Think about a fear that you have been avoiding. It can be anything from a fear of spiders to a fear of speaking in front of others.

Write down your fear below:

Fear: _____

_____

Now, let's break down your fear into smaller parts. Write down the specific situations or triggers that make you feel afraid:

Situation/Trigger 1: _____

Situation/Trigger 2: _____

Situation/Trigger 3: _____

Next, let's identify the thoughts and feelings you have when you face your fear. Write them down below:

Thoughts: _____

Feelings: _____

Now, let's challenge those thoughts. Are they based on facts or assumptions? Write down evidence that supports or disproves your thoughts:

Evidence for: _____

Evidence against: _____

After looking at the evidence, what is a more balanced thought you can have about the situation? Write it down below:

Balanced thought: _____

Finally, let's make a plan for facing your fear. Write down a specific goal that you can work towards and a plan for achieving it:

Goal: _____

Plan: _____

Remember to take things one step at a time and be kind to yourself throughout the process. Facing your fears can be challenging, but with CBT, you can learn to manage your anxiety and overcome avoidance behaviors.

Overcoming Distressing Thoughts

If you find yourself struggling with an upsetting thought, there are some inquiries you can make to determine whether or not it holds true. Jot down your distressing thought in the large cloud below and then explore the smaller clouds for questions to ask yourself.

Is there an alternative perspective to consider?

Is this thought based on facts or assumptions?

How is this thought serving me?

Challenge those negative thoughts and take control of your mind.

_____

_____

_____

Can I reframe this thought with a positive perspective?

How would someone else perceive this thought?

What guidance would I offer to a friend in this situation?

Facing My Fears

The "Facing My Fears" worksheet helps kids identify their fears and create a fear hierarchy based on the level of anxiety each fear provokes. The worksheet offers a step-by-step method for gradually introducing the child to situations that cause anxiety. The process begins with the least anxiety-inducing situation and progresses up the hierarchy with each successful exposure. By breaking down the fear into manageable steps and providing support from a trusted adult, this worksheet can help kids build confidence and overcome their fears.

Facing My Fears

Instructions: In the space provided, list your fears in order from the least scary to the scariest. Then, think of specific steps you can take to gradually face each fear, starting with the least scary.

Fear Hierarchy:

Steps to Face My Fears:

Fear # 1: _____

Step 1: _____

Step 2: _____

Step 3: _____

Fear # 2: _____

Step 1: _____

Step 2: _____

Step 3: _____

Fear # 3: _____

Step 1: _____

Step 2: _____

Step 3: _____

Continue listing steps for each fear on your hierarchy.

Bonus: *Choose one fear from your hierarchy and practice facing it this week with the support of a trusted adult. Remember to take it one step at a time and celebrate your progress.*

Fear Ladder for Children

Begin by making a list of things that worry or scare your child. Choose one fear to focus on this week. Create a series of tasks to complete over the next one or two weeks, and arrange the tasks from the least scary (0) to the most scary (10).

Step	Action	Rating
Step 6	Be the leader and ask a group of friends to play together	10
Step 5	Ask a friend to play with during recess	8
Step 4	Ask to sit with a friend during lunch	7
Step 3	Start a conversation with a friend by asking a question	5
Step 2	Greet three friends by saying hi	4
Step 1	Make eye contact with two of the least scary people around you	2

The Relaxation Techniques

"The Relaxation Techniques" worksheet helps children learn and practice different strategies to calm their minds and bodies when facing feared situations. By using techniques like deep breathing, progressive muscle relaxation, or visualization, children can learn to manage anxiety and feel more in control during exposure. By practicing these techniques regularly, children can develop a sense of self-efficacy and reduce their reliance on avoidance behaviors.

RELAXATION TECHNIQUES WORKSHEET

Instructions: In the space provided, practice the following relaxation techniques to help you feel calm and safe during exposure to feared situations. Choose the techniques that work best for you and make a plan to practice them regularly.

Deep Breathing

- Find a comfortable position and take a deep breath from your nose, counting to four.
- Hold your breath for a count of four.
- Slowly exhale from your mouth, counting to six.
- Repeat for several breaths, focusing on the sound and sensation of your breath.

Progressive Muscle Relaxation

- Tense a muscle group, such as your fists, for a count of 5.
- Release the tension and relax the muscles for a count of 10.
- Move to the next muscle group, such as your arms, and repeat.
- Continue tensing and releasing muscle groups until you have relaxed your entire body.

Visualization

- Close your eyes and imagine a peaceful scene, such as a beach or forest.
- Use your senses to picture the details of the scene, such as the sound of the waves or the smell of the trees.
- Focus on the sensations of relaxation and calmness that come with this visualization.

Mindfulness

- Bring your attention to the present moment, noticing the sensations in your body and your surroundings.
- Use your senses to focus on what you see, hear, smell, taste, and feel.
- Notice any thoughts or feelings that come up, but try to let them pass without judgment.

Bonus: *Choose one or two relaxation techniques from this worksheet and practice them daily for a week. Notice how they make you feel and how they can help you feel calm and safe during exposure to feared situations.*

Art Therapy

Utilizing creative expression to promote emotional healing and well-being, art therapy is a form of psychotherapy. Mindfulness for children is a technique that involves observing the present moment without criticism. When these two practices are merged, children can cultivate self-awareness, manage their emotions, and enhance their mental well-being. Along with Mindful practices, kids can color the picture below to achieve the desired outcomes.

Chapter 7: Building Positive Relationships with Your Child

Building positive relationships with your child involves creating a strong and healthy bond through effective communication, active listening, empathy, respect, and support. It also involves spending quality time together, engaging in shared activities, and creating positive memories. By performing therapy techniques and activities with their kids, you can build a positive relationship with your child. You can promote their emotional well-being, boost their self-esteem, and help them develop positive social skills and relationships with others.

7.1. Broken Bonds: How Childhood Trauma Can Damage Relationships in Adulthood

Childhood trauma can have a profound impact on adult relationships. Trauma can lead to attachment issues, trust issues, and difficulty forming and maintaining healthy relationships. Here are some examples of how childhood trauma can damage relationships in adulthood:

Attachment Issues: Trauma can cause children to develop attachment issues, such as avoidance or fear of intimacy. This can make it difficult for them to form close, healthy relationships as adults.

Trust Issues: Childhood trauma can cause individuals to struggle with trust, which can affect their ability to form and maintain *relationships. They may struggle to trust others, or they may be overly trusting and vulnerable to exploitation.*

Emotional Regulation: Trauma can also impact emotional regulation, making it difficult for individuals to manage their emotions in relationships. They may struggle with intense emotions, such as anger, fear, and sadness, which can make it difficult for them to connect with others.

Communication: Trauma can also affect communication skills, making it difficult for individuals to express their needs and emotions effectively. This can lead to misunderstandings and conflicts in relationships.

Role Modeling: Finally, childhood trauma can impact individuals' ability to be positive role model in their relationships. If they did not have positive role models growing up, they may struggle to model healthy behaviors and may repeat the negative patterns they learned in childhood.

Overall, childhood trauma can have a lasting impact on adult relationships, making it important for individuals to seek help and support in overcoming the effects of trauma.

7.2. Building Positive Relationships with Your Child

Building positive relationships with your child involves creating a strong bond based on trust, love, and communication. Some ways to achieve this include:

Spending quality time together: Making time for your child and participating in activities they enjoy can help strengthen your bond and build positive memories.

Active listening: Paying attention to your child's thoughts, feelings, and experiences can help them feel heard and validated, strengthening your communication and relationship.

Positive reinforcement: Acknowledging your child's positive behavior, efforts, and accomplishments can help boost their confidence and self-esteem, creating a positive dynamic in your relationship.

Establishing boundaries: Setting clear boundaries and rules can help your child feel safe and secure while also promoting mutual respect in your relationship.

Empathy and understanding: Recognizing and responding to your child's emotions with empathy and understanding can help build trust and foster a deeper connection in your relationship. For example, regularly spending time playing games, reading books, or going on outings with your child can create positive memories and strengthen your bond.

Active listening can involve putting away distractions and fully engaging in conversations with your child to understand their thoughts and feelings. Positive reinforcement can be as simple as offering praise for a job well done or celebrating achievements together. Establishing boundaries might involve setting a limitation or discussing household rules together, while empathy and understanding can be shown by validating your child's feelings and offering support during difficult times.

7.3. Developing Healthy Boundaries

Developing healthy boundaries is an essential aspect of building positive relationships with your child. It involves setting limits and expectations for behavior while respecting your child's individuality and personal space. Here are some ways to develop healthy boundaries with your child:

Communicate: *Talk to your child openly and honestly about your expectations, rules, and consequences. Listen to their thoughts and feelings, and try to find a compromise that works for both of you.*

Be consistent: *Once you set boundaries, be consistent in enforcing them. This helps your child understand what is expected of them and reinforces the importance of respecting boundaries.*

Respect their privacy: *As your child grows, they may want more privacy. Respect their need for personal space, and teach them to respect the privacy of others as well.*

Encourage independence: *Allow your child to make age-appropriate decisions and take responsibility for their actions. This helps them develop a sense of independence and self-reliance.*

Be flexible: *It's important to be firm with boundaries but also be willing to adjust them as needed. As your child grows and develops, their needs and abilities will change, and so should your boundaries.*

Examples of healthy boundaries might include setting a limit for your teenager, enforcing consequences for disrespectful behavior, respecting your child's need for alone time, and encouraging them to make decisions for themselves within a set of agreed-upon guidelines. Ultimately, developing healthy boundaries helps your child feel safe, respected, and loved, which can lead to a stronger and more positive relationship.

7.4. Ventures

My Support System

The "My Support System" worksheet helps kids identify individuals who provide them with support and comfort. By recognizing these people, children can build and strengthen their social support network, which can have a positive impact on their mental health and well-being. This worksheet can also help children develop positive relationships and improve their communication skills. Additionally, identifying supportive people and ways to connect with them can help children feel less alone and more empowered to seek help when needed.

My Support System

Instructions: In the space provided, identify the people in your life who are supportive and helpful, and think about how you can connect with them when you need support.

Who are the supportive people in your life?

- List the names of people you feel comfortable talking to about your feelings and experiences.
- Think about family members, friends, teachers, coaches, or counselors who have been there for you in the past.

_____

_____

_____

_____

What kind of support do they offer?

- Write down what each supportive person can offer you in terms of emotional, practical, or other types of support.
- For example, a friend might be a good listener, while a family member might offer advice or help with tasks.

_____

_____

_____

How can you connect with them?

- Think about ways to reach out to your supportive people when you need help or just want to talk.
- Write down their phone numbers, email addresses, or social media profiles.

_____

_____

_____

_____

- Brainstorm specific activities you can do together, such as going for a walk or watching a movie.

_____

_____

_____

_____

What other sources of support do you have?

- Consider other sources of support, such as pets, hobbies, or online communities.
- Write down how these sources of support can help you feel better when you're feeling down.

_____

_____

_____

_____

_____

Bonus: *Choose one supportive person from your list and think about what you can do to strengthen your connection with them. Make a plan to reach out to them and spend time together.*

Building Positive Relationships

The "Building Positive Relationships" worksheet is an important tool for parents and caregivers who want to strengthen their relationship with their child through CBT. It provides a structured approach for identifying communication patterns, challenging negative thoughts, setting goals and actions, and reinforcing positive behaviors. By using this worksheet, parents and caregivers can improve the quality of their relationship with their child, which can have a positive impact on their mental health and well-being.

Building Positive Relationships (For Parents)

Instructions:

Take a few minutes to think about your relationship with your child. What are some of the things you appreciate about your child? What are some areas where you would like to improve your relationship? Write down your thoughts below:

Appreciations: _____

_____

Areas for improvement: _____

_____

_____

Now, let's focus on communication. Good communication is the foundation of a strong relationship. Write down some of the ways you communicate with your child:

Communication methods: _____

_____

_____

_____

Next, let's explore your thoughts and feelings when you communicate with your child. Write down your thoughts and feelings during the following scenarios:

Scenario 1: When your child doesn't listen to you.

Thoughts: _____

_____

Feelings: _____

_____

Scenario 2: When you are feeling stressed or overwhelmed.

Thoughts: _____

_____

Feelings: _____

_____

Let's challenge those negative thoughts. Are they based on facts or assumptions? Write down evidence that supports or disproves your thoughts:

Evidence for: _____

Evidence against: _____

After looking at the evidence, what is a more balanced thought you can have about the situation? Write it down below:

Balanced thought: _____

Now, let's make a plan for improving communication with your child. Write down some specific goals and actions you can take:

Goal 1: _____

Action: _____

Goal 2: _____

Action: _____

Finally, let's talk about how to reinforce positive behaviors in your child. Write down some of your child's positive qualities and behaviors that you want to encourage:

Positive qualities: _____

Positive behaviors: _____

Write down some specific ways you can reinforce positive behaviors:

Ways to reinforce positive behaviors: _____

_____

_____

_____

Remember, building positive relationships takes time and effort. By using CBT techniques, you can learn to communicate effectively with your child, challenge negative thoughts, and reinforce positive behaviors.

Setting Boundaries

The "Setting Boundaries" worksheet is a valuable tool for helping kids learn to set and communicate healthy boundaries. This worksheet provides a structured approach for kids to identify their own boundaries, practice expressing them to others, and learn how to respect the boundaries of others. By working through this worksheet, kids can gain a better understanding of their own needs and limits, as well as develop important skills for building positive relationships with others. This can lead to increased confidence, self-esteem, and overall well-being.

Setting Boundaries

Instructions: In the space provided, practice setting and communicating healthy boundaries with others, and learn how to respect others' boundaries.

Identify your boundaries

- Think about the things that make you feel uncomfortable, disrespected, or unsafe.
- Write down your boundaries in specific terms. For example, "I don't want people to touch me without my permission" or "I don't want to be called names or insulted."

_____

_____

_____

Communicate your boundaries

- Think about how you can communicate your boundaries clearly and assertively.
- Practice saying "no" or "stop" in a firm but respectful tone.
- Brainstorm ways to explain why you have a particular boundary. For example, "I don't like being tickled because it makes me feel anxious."

_____

_____

_____

Respect others' boundaries

- Think about the boundaries that other people might have and how you can respect them.
- Practice listening to others and paying attention to their body language and tone of voice.
- Ask for permission before touching someone, and avoid making assumptions about what they might be comfortable with.

_____

_____

_____

Consequences for boundary violations

- Think about what you can do if someone violates your boundaries and how you can enforce consequences in a respectful way.
- Practice saying things like, "I've asked you to stop, and if you don't respect my boundary, I will have to leave the situation."
- Think about what kind of consequences are appropriate for different boundary violations. For example, if someone calls you a name, you might ask them to apologize, while if someone touches you without your permission, you might need to involve an adult.

_____

_____

_____

_____

Bonus: *Think about a situation where you might need to set a boundary in the future and practice what you might say to communicate your boundary assertively and respectfully.*

Chapter 8: Encouraging Your Child's Self-Care and Self-Compassion

Encouraging your child's self-care and self-compassion involves teaching them to prioritize their own physical, emotional, and mental health. This can include practicing activities that promote relaxation, self-expression, and mindfulness. Additionally, it involves teaching them to be kind and understanding towards themselves, acknowledging their strengths, and accepting their limitations. Promoting self-care and self-compassion can be an effective way to help children who have experienced trauma to develop greater self-esteem, resilience, and emotional regulation, and to build positive coping skills.

Parents can encourage self-compassion in their children through the use of the CBT technique. In cognitive therapy, self-compassion means examining negative and automatic self-critical thoughts and challenging those thoughts. To help children come to terms with both their positive and negative feelings, parents can understand and validate their experiences and emotions and avoid being dismissive of their feelings. By teaching children CBT techniques, parents can help their children develop self-care and self-compassion skills that can benefit their mental health and well-being. Moreover, CBT encourages gratitude and positive thinking, which can improve a child's mood and overall well-being. By encouraging children to identify things they are grateful for and focus on the positive aspects of their life, parents can help them develop a more positive outlook and reduce negative self-talk.

8.1. The Importance of Self-Care and Self-Compassion

Self-care and self-compassion are crucial for the overall well-being and development of children. Here are some reasons why:

> o *Promotes positive self-esteem*: When children practice self-care, they learn to value and respect themselves. This helps to build a positive self-image and self-esteem, which in turn can lead to better mental health outcomes.
>
> o *Encourages self-awareness:* Self-care and self-compassion encourage children to be aware of their own needs and feelings. This helps them to better understand their emotions and communicate them effectively to others.
>
> o *Reduces stress and anxiety*: Self-care practices such as mindfulness, meditation, or physical exercise can help children to manage stress and anxiety. By taking time for self-care, children learn to prioritize their own well-being and develop healthy coping mechanisms.
>
> o *Fosters resilience*: When children practice self-care and self-compassion, they develop resilience in the face of challenges and setbacks. They learn to be kind and patient with themselves, which helps them to bounce back from difficult situations.

Examples of self-care and self-compassion practices for children include taking breaks when feeling overwhelmed, engaging in physical activity or creative hobbies, practicing mindfulness or meditation, and talking to a trusted adult or friend when feeling stressed or anxious. By encouraging and modeling these practices, parents can help their children develop healthy self-care habits and improve their overall well-being.

8.2. Developing A Self-Care Plan with Your Child

Developing a self-care plan with your child is an important step in encouraging self-care and self-compassion. It involves identifying activities and practices that promote well-being and incorporating them into daily routines. Here are some steps to develop a self-care plan with your child:

o *Identify self-care activities*: Talk with your child about activities that make them feel happy, calm, and energized. This could include things like drawing, playing with a pet, and reading, listening to music, or taking a walk.

o *Prioritize activities*: Once you have identified self-care activities, help your child prioritize them based on what is most important or beneficial for their well-being.

o *Schedule self-care activities*: Help your child schedule self-care activities into their daily routine. This could mean setting aside time in the morning or evening or finding opportunities to incorporate self-care activities throughout the day.

o *Create reminders*: Encourage your child to create reminders or visual cues to help them remember to practice self-care. This could be a sticky note on their mirror or a reminder on their phone.

o *Adjust and revise as needed*: Check in with your child regularly to see how their self-care plan is working and adjust or revise it as needed.

Examples of self-care activities for children could include:

o Taking a bath or shower
o Practicing deep breathing or relaxation techniques
o Doing yoga or stretching
o Drawing or coloring

- o Playing with a pet
- o Listening to music
- o Spending time in nature
- o Reading a book
- o Writing or journaling
- o Spending time with friends or family

By developing a self-care plan with your child, you can help them prioritize their well-being and develop healthy habits for life.

8.3. Encouraging Self-Compassion in Your Child

Encouraging self-compassion in children is important for their mental health and well-being. Here are some ways parents can promote self-compassion in their children:

Validate their feelings: When your child is going through a difficult time, it is important to acknowledge their emotions and validate their feelings. Help them to understand that it is okay to feel sad, angry, or anxious sometimes.

Be kind to yourself: Children learn by example, so it is important for parents to model self-compassion themselves. This means being kind to yourself and not being too hard on yourself when things go wrong.

Encourage positive self-talk: Encourage your child to use positive self-talk and to be kind to themselves. Help them to reframe negative thoughts into positive ones.

Celebrate small victories: Take time to acknowledge and celebrate any minor accomplishments of your child, as it will enhance their sense of self-assurance and self-worth.

Encourage self-care: Motivate your child to take part in activities that they enjoy and find relaxing, like physical activities, reading, or spending time with friends. Assist them in giving importance to self-care as a crucial element of their everyday regimen.

Teach coping skills: Teach your child coping skills to help them manage stress and difficult emotions. These may include deep breathing, mindfulness, or journaling.

Practice empathy: Help your child to understand and practice empathy towards others. This can help them to develop a greater sense of compassion for themselves and others.

Examples of promoting self-compassion in children include encouraging them to take breaks when they need to, teaching them to celebrate their strengths, and helping them to understand that making mistakes is a normal part of the learning process. Additionally, parents can teach children to be kind to themselves when they are struggling and to practice self-care activities such as taking a bubble bath or going for a walk in nature. Ultimately, promoting self-compassion in children can help them to build resilience, manage stress, and lead happier, healthier lives.

8.4. Ventures
My Self-Care Plan

The "My Self-Care Plan" worksheet is a helpful tool for kids to identify self-care practices that work best for them. It allows children to explore their interests, hobbies, and ways to manage stress or negative emotions. By creating a self-care plan, children can develop a routine that promotes well-being, resilience, and self-compassion. The worksheet also helps children to take ownership of their self-care and recognize the importance of prioritizing their mental and emotional health.

My Self-Care Plan

Instructions: Use this worksheet to create a plan for taking care of yourself and staying healthy and happy.

Self-Care Activities: List some activities that you enjoy doing and that help you feel relaxed and happy. These can be simple things like taking a bath, listening to music, or going for a walk.

Activity Ideas:

- Reading a book

- Drawing or coloring

- Playing a game

- Taking a nap

- Dancing

- Doing a puzzle

- Cooking or baking

- Watching a movie

Coping Strategies: Write down some ways you can cope with difficult emotions or situations. These can be things like taking deep breaths, talking to a friend or family member, or going for a run.

Coping Strategies:

- Deep breathing exercises

- Talking to a trusted friend or family member

- Writing in a journal

- Going for a walk or run

- Meditating or practicing mindfulness

- Doing something creative, like painting or playing music

Relaxation Techniques: Think of some relaxation techniques that work for you, like taking a warm bath, practicing yoga, or listening to calming music.

Relaxation Techniques:

- Taking a warm bath

- Practicing yoga or stretching

- Listening to calming music or nature sounds

- Visualizing a peaceful place

- Doing a body scan meditation

- Using a weighted blanket or cuddling with a pet

Healthy Habits: List some healthy habits that you want to incorporate into your daily routine, like eating nutritious foods, getting enough sleep, or exercising regularly.

Healthy Habits:

- Eating a balanced diet with lots of fruits and vegetables

- Drinking plenty of water

- Getting enough sleep each night

- Exercising regularly, like going for a walk or bike ride

- Spending time outside in nature

- Limiting screen time and unplugging before bedtime

Self-Care Plan: Use the information you've gathered to create a self-care plan that works for you. Write down some specific activities or strategies you can use when you need to take care of yourself.

_____

_____

_____

_____

_____

_____

_____

Suggested Self-Care Plan:

- On weekdays, I will go for a walk after school to get some fresh air and exercise.

- Before bed each night, I will spend 10 minutes doing a relaxation exercise like deep breathing or a body scan meditation.

- When I feel overwhelmed or stressed, I will take a break and do something creative, like drawing or painting.

- If I have a hard time falling asleep, I will listen to calming music or a guided meditation.

- I will drink water throughout the day to stay hydrated and energized.

Remember, it's important to take care of yourself and prioritize your well-being. Use this worksheet as a guide to create a self-care plan that works for you, and remember to practice self-care regularly.

Practicing Self-Care and Self-Compassion

The "Practicing Self-Care and Self-Compassion" worksheet is an important tool for children and adolescents who are learning to prioritize their own well-being through CBT. It helps them define and explore self-care and self-compassion practices, challenge negative thoughts, set goals and actions, and reinforce positive behaviors. Through utilizing this worksheet, children and adolescents can cultivate positive practices and enhance their psychological wellness and overall state of being.

Practicing Self-Care
and Self-Compassion

Instructions:

Let's start by defining self-care and self-compassion. Write down your own definition for each:

Self-care: _____

Self-compassion: _____

Now, let's explore how you practice self-care and self-compassion in your own life. Write down some examples of self-care and self-compassion practices you use:

Self-care practices: _____

Self-compassion practices: _____

Next, let's talk about your child's self-care and self-compassion practices. Write down some of the ways your child takes care of themselves and shows self-compassion:

Self-care practices: _____

Self-compassion practices: _____

Now, let's look at some common negative thoughts your child might have about themselves. Write down any negative thoughts your child has expressed or that you have observed:

Negative thoughts: _____

Let's challenge those negative thoughts. Are they based on facts or assumptions? Write down evidence that supports or disproves those thoughts:

Evidence for: _____

Evidence against: _____

After looking at the evidence, what is a more balanced thought your child can have about themselves? Write it down below:

Balanced thought: _____

Now, let's make a plan for practicing self-care and self-compassion. Write down some specific goals and actions your child can take:

Goal 1: _____

Action: _____

Goal 2: _____

Action: _____

Finally, let's talk about how to reinforce self-care and self-compassion practices. Write down some specific ways you can encourage and support your child:

Ways to reinforce self-care and self-compassion practices:

_____

Remember, practicing self-care and self-compassion is an ongoing process. By using CBT techniques, your child can learn to challenge negative thoughts and build positive self-care and self-compassion habits.

Self-Compassion Exercises

The "Self-Compassion Exercises" can be a helpful tool for kids to practice treating themselves with kindness and understanding. It provides various exercises for them to try, such as writing a letter to themselves or creating a self-compassion mantra, which can help them develop a positive self-image and cope with difficult emotions. By practicing self-compassion, kids can learn to be more patient and forgiving with themselves, which can ultimately lead to greater self-esteem and resilience.

Self-Compassion Exercises

Instructions: Self-compassion involves treating ourselves with kindness and understanding, especially when we're struggling or feeling down. Try these exercises to practice self-compassion.

Writing a Letter to Yourself: Write a letter to yourself as if you were writing to a friend who is going through a hard time. Use words of encouragement and support, and remind yourself of your strengths and abilities.

Self-Compassion Mantra: Choose a phrase or mantra that helps you feel calm and grounded. Examples include "I am worthy of love and kindness" or "May I be kind to myself at this moment." Repeat this mantra to yourself when you need a reminder to be compassionate towards yourself.

Acknowledging Emotions: When you're feeling strong emotions, take a moment to acknowledge them without judgment. Say to yourself, "It's okay to feel this way right now," or "I'm allowed to have these feelings." This can help you feel more accepting of yourself and your emotions.

LETTER TO ME FROM ME

Mindful Breathing: Take a few deep breaths, and focus your attention on your breath. Notice the sensation of the air entering and leaving your body. As you inhale, think, "I am breathing in calm." As you exhale, think, "I am breathing out stress."

Self-Hug: Wrap your arms around yourself in a gentle hug, and imagine sending yourself feelings of warmth and comfort. This can help you feel more connected to yourself and soothe difficult emotions.

Remember, practicing self-compassion takes time and patience. Be kind and gentle with yourself as you try these exercises.

Positive Self-Talk

Positive self-talk and self-compassion are closely linked. Research has shown that positive self- talk improves health, relationships, motivation, self-confidence and resilience. It also improves mental and physical well-being. Here is an activity help your kid improve their self-talk.

CONFIDENT SELF-TALK

1. Identify the positive and supportive messages that resonate with you and that you want to remember and apply for positive self-talk.

2. Create a visual representation of yourself or an object that symbolizes your personality or character in the center of the mirror to serve as a reminder of your unique qualities.

3. Speak the positive self-talk statements out loud to yourself regularly to reinforce their empowering message and boost your confidence and self-belief.

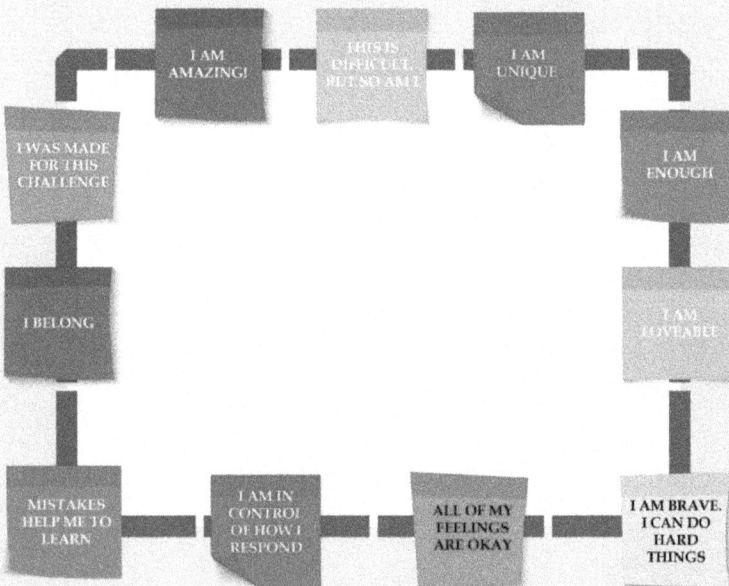

I AM AMAZING!

THIS IS DIFFICULT, BUT SO AM I

I AM UNIQUE

I WAS MADE FOR THIS CHALLENGE

I AM ENOUGH

I BELONG

I AM LOVEABLE

MISTAKES HELP ME TO LEARN

I AM IN CONTROL OF HOW I RESPOND

ALL OF MY FEELINGS ARE OKAY

I AM BRAVE. I CAN DO HARD THINGS

Chapter 9: Moving Forward with Your Child's Healing

Moving forward with your child's healing involves creating a supportive environment, fostering resilience, and seeking professional help if necessary. This includes providing ongoing emotional support, building coping skills, promoting positive relationships, and encouraging self-care and self-compassion. It also involves recognizing that healing is a process and that progress may be slow and non-linear. With patience, empathy, and a commitment to your child's well-being, you can help them move towards a brighter future.

CBT can help parents and their children move forward in the healing journey by using goal-setting, problem-solving, positive thinking, mindfulness, and self-care techniques. By breaking down goals into smaller steps, developing problem-solving skills, challenging negative self-talk, practicing mindfulness, and engaging in self-care activities, children can learn to manage their emotions, set goals, and promote positive thinking. CBT provides practical and goal-oriented approaches to promote positive change and support children in their healing journey.

9.1. Celebrating Progress with Your Child

Recognizing and celebrating progress is an important part of helping children recover from trauma. It can provide motivation and encouragement to continue their healing journey. Here are some ways to celebrate progress with your child:

- ○ **Acknowledge and validate their efforts**: Show your child that you recognize and appreciate the hard work they are putting in to overcome their trauma. Validate their progress and express your pride in them.
- ○ **Celebrate milestones:** Set achievable goals with your child and celebrate when they reach them. It can be as simple as celebrating when they share their feelings or try a new activity.
- ○ **Use a progress chart**: Visual aids like progress charts can help your child see how far they have come and give them a sense of accomplishment.
- ○ **Reward them:** Small rewards can be a great way to recognize your child's hard work. Rewards can be as simple as a special treat or a fun activity.
- ○ **Celebrate together as a family**: Celebrating your child's progress as a family can create a sense of togetherness and support.

For example, if your child has a fear of dogs and has been working on overcoming it, you can celebrate their progress by taking them to a petting zoo where they can interact with animals in a safe and controlled environment. You can also acknowledge their efforts by telling them how proud you are of them and how much progress they have made.

Remember that celebrating progress is not about achieving perfection. It's about acknowledging the small steps your child takes toward healing and growth.

9.2. Setting Goals for The Future with Your Child

Setting goals for the future with your child can be an important part of their trauma-healing journey. Here are some ways to approach this:

- o **Start with small goals:** *It can be helpful to begin with small, achievable goals that your child can work towards. This can help build their confidence and motivation.*
- o **Discuss interests and aspirations:** *Talk to your child about their interests and aspirations and how they might like to pursue them. This can help them develop a sense of purpose and direction.*
- o **Make a plan:** *Work with your child to create a plan for achieving their goals. This can include breaking down larger goals into smaller steps and identifying any obstacles or challenges that may need to be addressed.*
- o **Celebrate successes**: *Celebrate your child's successes along the way, no matter how small. This can help reinforce positive behaviors and motivate them to continue working towards their goals.*
- o **Be flexible**: *It's important to be flexible and adjust the plan as needed. Trauma healing is not always a linear process, and setbacks may occur. It's important to be supportive and encourage your child to keep moving forward.*

Examples of goals could include academic achievements, extracurricular activities, social events, and personal growth, such as developing new skills or hobbies. The key is to identify goals that are important to your child and help them move towards a more positive and fulfilling future.

9.3. Planning for Potential Setbacks

Planning for potential setbacks is an important aspect of moving forward with your child's trauma healing. It involves anticipating potential obstacles or challenges that your child may face in the future and developing a plan for how to overcome them.

Here are some steps you can take to plan for potential setbacks:

- o **Identify potential triggers or stressors:** *Think about the situations or events that may trigger negative emotions or memories for your child. These could be things like anniversaries of traumatic events, certain people or places, or specific activities.*
- o **Develop a plan for how to handle these triggers**: *Once you've identified potential triggers, work with your child to develop a plan for how to handle them. This might involve practicing relaxation techniques, talking to a trusted adult or therapist, or engaging in a positive distraction.*
- o **Encourage open communication:** *Encourage your child to communicate openly with you about their feelings and experiences. Let them know that it's okay to have setbacks and that you're there to support them through the healing process.*
- o **Revisit goals and strategies**: *Periodically revisit the goals and strategies that you and your child have developed together. Make adjustments as needed, and celebrate the progress that your child has made.*

Here's an example: Let's say that your child experienced a traumatic event at a park and now feels anxious and fearful whenever they go to a park. You might work with your child to develop a plan for how to handle this trigger. This could involve practicing deep breathing and visualization techniques and having a trusted adult or therapist accompany your child to the park. You might also encourage your child to communicate openly with you about their feelings and celebrate small steps forward, such as visiting a park with a therapist or trusted adult. If your child experiences a setback, you might revisit the plan and make adjustments as needed, such as practicing relaxation techniques more frequently or seeking additional support from a therapist.

9.4. Ventures

My Goals

The "My Goals" worksheet is designed to help children set short-term and long-term goals for their healing journey and identify specific steps they can take to achieve them. By using this worksheet, children can learn the importance of setting goals and develop a sense of control over their own healing process. This worksheet can also help children build confidence and motivation as they work towards achieving their goals.

My Goals

Instructions: Think about what you want to achieve on your healing journey. Write down your short-term and long-term goals, and identify the steps you can take to achieve them.

Short-term goals (within the next week or month):

Goal 1:_____

Steps I can take to achieve this goal:

_____

_____

_____

_____

_____

Goal 2: _____

Steps I can take to achieve this goal:

_____

_____

_____

_____

_____

Long-term goals (within the next six months to a year):

Goal 1:_____

Steps I can take to achieve this goal:

_____

_____

_____

_____

_____

Goal 2: _____

Steps I can take to achieve this goal:

_____

_____

_____

_____

_____

Remember, it's okay if your goals change over time. The important thing is to have something to work towards and celebrate your progress along the way!

Moving Forward with Your Child's Healing

The "Moving Forward with Your Child's Healing" worksheet is an important tool for parents and caregivers who are supporting their child's mental health through CBT. It provides a structured approach for reflecting on progress and setbacks, challenging negative thoughts, setting goals and actions, and reinforcing positive changes. By using this worksheet, parents and caregivers can continue to support their child's healing and progress towards improved mental health and well-being.

Moving Forward with Your Child's Healing

Instructions:

Take a few minutes to reflect on your child's progress so far. What positive changes have you noticed in your child's behavior or mood since starting CBT? Write them down below:

Positive changes: _____

Now, let's talk about any challenges your child has faced in the healing process. Write down any obstacles or setbacks your child has experienced:

Obstacles: _____

Setbacks: _____

Let's explore any negative thoughts or beliefs that might be holding your child back. Write down any negative thoughts your child has expressed or that you have observed:

Negative thoughts: _____

Let's challenge those negative thoughts. Are they based on facts or assumptions? Write down evidence that supports or disproves those thoughts:

Evidence for: _____

Evidence against: _____

After looking at the evidence, what is a more balanced thought your child can have about themselves and their progress? Write it down below:

Balanced thought: _____

Let's make a plan for moving forward with your child's healing. Write down some specific goals and actions you and your child can take:

Goal 1: _____

Action: _____

Goal 2: _____

Action: _____

Finally, let's talk about how you can reinforce positive changes and behaviors in your child. Write down some specific ways you can encourage and support your child:

Ways to reinforce positive changes: _____

_____

_____

_____

Remember, healing is a process that takes time and effort. By using CBT techniques and setting specific goals and actions, you and your child can continue to make progress and move forward in the healing process.

Celebrating Progress

The "Celebrating Progress" worksheet helps children by encouraging them to reflect on the progress they have made in their healing journey. By acknowledging their achievements, children can build their self-esteem and motivation to continue their healing work. This worksheet also helps children identify areas where they still need support and growth, allowing them to set new goals and continue moving forward. Ultimately, this worksheet helps children stay focused on their journey of healing and encourages them to celebrate their successes along the way.

Celebrating Progress

Instructions: Use this worksheet to reflect on your progress in your healing journey and celebrate your accomplishments. Take time to appreciate your hard work and the progress you have made, and identify areas where you still need support and growth.

Reflect on your journey so far. What are some of the challenges you have faced, and how have you overcome them?

_____

_____

Write down some of the things you have accomplished since starting your healing journey. These can be big or small achievements, such as trying a new coping strategy or talking about your feelings with a trusted adult.

_____

_____

Think about the people who have supported you along the way. Who have been there for you, listened to you, and encouraged you? Write down their names and how they have helped you.

_____

_____

Identify areas where you still need support and growth. What are some of the things you would like to work on or improve? Think about what resources or strategies could help you in these areas.

_____

_____

Finally, take time to celebrate your progress and accomplishments. You can do this by treating yourself to something special, doing something you enjoy, or simply acknowledging your hard work and determination. Remember that healing is a journey, and every step forward is worth celebrating.

Reflection Questions:

What are some of the accomplishments that you are proudest of?

_____

_____

_____

Who has been the biggest support for you during your healing journey?

_____

_____

_____

What are some areas where you still need support or growth?

_____

_____

_____

How can you celebrate your progress and continue to work towards your goals?

_____

_____

_____

Conclusion

Childhood trauma can have a major impact on a person's life, but it doesn't have to define their future. "The Childhood Trauma Workbook for Kids" is a valuable resource for children who have experienced trauma and are looking for ways to heal and move forward in their lives. This workbook utilizes evidence-based Cognitive Behavioral Therapy (CBT) techniques to guide children through the process of understanding and managing their trauma-related symptoms. With interactive worksheets, activities, and exercises, children are empowered to take an active role in their healing journey. They are encouraged to explore their emotions, identify triggers, and develop coping strategies to manage their symptoms. The workbook also emphasizes the significance of self-care, self-compassion, and building positive relationships.

Through the use of relatable examples and engaging exercises, children are able to gain a better understanding of their trauma and how it has impacted their lives. They are guided through a process of healing and self-discovery, helping them to move from surviving to thriving. Overall, "The Childhood Trauma Workbook for Kids 9-12" provides a comprehensive and empowering guideline for the parents to help their children overcome their past wounds and develop the tools necessary for a fulfilling and resilient future. This workbook is a must-have for any parent whose child has experienced trauma and is looking to take control of their healing journey.

www.ingramcontent.com/pod-product-compliance
Lightning Source LLC
Chambersburg PA
CBHW052117030426
42335CB00025B/3018